SARAH PALIN

Recent Titles in Greenwood Biographies

SARAH PALIN

A Biography

Carolyn Kraemer Cooper

GREENWOOD BIOGRAPHIES

 GREENWOOD

AN IMPRINT OF ABC-CLIO, LLC
Santa Barbara, California • Denver, Colorado • Oxford, England

Library of Congress Cataloging-in-Publication Data

Cooper, Carolyn Kraemer
   Sarah Palin : a biography / Carolyn Kraemer Cooper.
      p. cm. — (Greenwood biographies)
   Includes bibliographical references and index.
   ISBN 978-0-313-37738-9 (hard copy : alk. paper) —
ISBN 978-0-313-37739-6 (ebook)   1. Palin, Sarah, 1964–   2. Women
governors—Alaska—Biography.   3. Governors—Alaska—Biography.
4. Women politicians—Alaska—Biography.   5. Women politicians—
United States—Biography.   6. Alaska—Politics and government—1959–
7. Vice-Presidential candidates—United States—Biography.   8. Presidents—
United States—Election—2008.   I. Title.

   F910.7.P35C67   2010
   973.931092—dc22
   [B]   2010032466

ISBN: 978-0-313-37738-9
EISBN: 978-0-313-37739-6

15   14   13   12   11   1   2   3   4   5

This book is also available on the World Wide Web as an eBook.
Visit www.abc-clio.com for details.

Greenwood
An Imprint of ABC-CLIO, LLC

ABC-CLIO, LLC
130 Cremona Drive, P.O. Box 1911
Santa Barbara, California 93116-1911

This book is printed on acid-free paper ∞

Manufactured in the United States of America

To Erica Cooper, my brave and fearless daughter, a future leader and moving force in computer research, who has unfailingly encouraged all of my creative efforts

CONTENTS

SERIES FOREWORD

In response to high school and public library needs, Greenwood developed this distinguished series of full-length biographies specifically for student use. Prepared by field experts and professionals, these engaging biographies are tailored for high school students who need challenging yet accessible biographies. Ideal for secondary school assignments, the length, format and subject areas are designed to meet educators' requirements and students' interests.

Greenwood offers an extensive selection of biographies spanning all curriculum related subject areas including social studies, the sciences, literature and the arts, history and politics, as well as popular culture, covering public figures and famous personalities from all time periods and backgrounds, both historic and contemporary, who have made an impact on American and/or world culture. Greenwood biographies were chosen based on comprehensive feedback from librarians and educators. Consideration was given to both curriculum relevance and inherent interest. The result is an intriguing mix of the well known and the unexpected, the saints and sinners from long-ago history and contemporary pop culture. Readers will find a wide array of subject choices from fascinating crime figures like Al Capone to inspiring pioneers like Margaret Mead, from the greatest minds of our time like Stephen Hawking to the most amazing success stories of our day like J. K. Rowling.

While the emphasis is on fact, not glorification, the books are meant to be fun to read. Each volume provides in-depth information about the subject's life from birth through childhood, the teen years, and adulthood. A thorough account relates family background and education, traces personal and professional influences, and explores struggles, accomplishments, and contributions. A timeline highlights the most significant life events against a historical perspective. Bibliographies supplement the reference value of each volume.

ACKNOWLEDGMENTS

Without the assistance of helpful and inspiring friends and colleagues, this book would not have come into print. First and foremost, many thanks to my most insightful editor, Sandy Towers of ABC-CLIO, who has pointed the way along the path to presenting a unified and hope-fully informative manuscript. Erica Cooper, my daughter, to whom this book is dedicated, has always provided the uplifting and inspiring light along the path in my darkest moments, especially when stranded in a snowstorm in Seattle en route to Anchorage.

Special thanks to Barbara S. Green for many years of encourage-ment in all my creative endeavors and to Marie Young for friendship and encouragement during the writing of this book. My appreciation goes to Irwin M. Goldberg for assisting with a journalist's approach to obtaining interviews, to Anna Chase for her probing and challenging insights, which helped to focus various parts of the book, and to Dr. Fred Anderson for historical pointers.

Special thanks to the McCain/Palin campaign staff in Arlington, Virginia, for providing access to telephone press conferences and press access to the Lancaster, Pennsylvania, Campaign Rally on October 18, 2008. My gratitude to John Cummins of the Arlington, Virginia,

Communications Department for the McCain/Palin Campaign for his support and interest in this project from its initiation.

   To the staff of the Marist College Library, especially Pepper Boetcker, head of Instruction and Extension Services, for assistance in locating source materials throughout the writing of this book, many thanks. Thanks, too, to Laura Fess for sharing her political ideas. My appreciation for support and encouragement in my professional development goes to Dr. Fiona Paton of the SUNY New Paltz English Department.

INTRODUCTION

The story of the life of Sarah Palin is one that extends far beyond the stereotypical rags to riches journey and in some ways approaches mythic proportions. In a modern climate that supports political leaders who have Ivy League educations, great wealth acquired through inheritance or personal effort, as well as vast and far-reaching political connections, it has been refreshing to see a woman who unconventionally worked her way through school by attending five colleges in an effort to receive her bachelor's degree, whose political connections began at the local gym, and whose image of an ordinary hockey mom was the persona she chose to present while running for vice president of the United States in 2008. She emerged on the national political stage full force in a day when few women have cracked the glass ceiling to the highest levels of political achievement.

When we think of Abraham Lincoln walking miles to school to receive an education and recall his early life in a log cabin, we can compare Sarah Palin's early childhood in her parents' home where her bedroom was heated only by a wood-burning stove, her necessity to take on brutal work as a salmon fisher during college summers, and her need to parade her beauty in what some consider to be demeaning pageants to earn tuition money for college, we see a populist in the making, a woman who understands the nature of hard work and humiliation and who climbs out of the Alaskan tundra onto the national scene in a burst of lightening, suddenly, and under fire from all quarters.

The tone in the United States during the 2008 presidential campaign regarding Sarah Palin was that of outrage. "How dare she!" was the general outcry, a person with limited education, fewer resources, and a woman to boot, presume to step up to the second most responsible job in American government. Her detractors, including political opponents, some members of the press, film stars, and television comics, focused on her wardrobe, her colloquial manner of speaking, her eyeglasses, and the fact that she lives in Alaska, the remotest state of the Union somewhat removed from the mainland, and presumably, therefore, its real concerns.

Some reporters attempted to intimidate, trick, and discredit her in interviews and in their presentation of her political views as well. Yet Palin kept right on going, making the rounds of political rallies across the country with enthusiasm and an all-American nationalistic spirit, and she enlivened John McCain's campaign for the presidency with her vibrant energy. At the very least, she gave her opponents a run for their money; at best, she paved the way for young women across the nation to realize their own potential in American politics.

Many times she stood up under attack; at others she faltered. However, she never backed down and waited patiently until the campaign was over to express her own outrage at the manner in which she had been treated. As a woman with a journalistic background, Palin understood the motivations of some members of the press. Many voters were shocked at the discrepancy in the way she had been presented to the nation as compared with her Democratic opponents. Photos of her head attached to seminude bodies were posted on the Internet and in the newsstand tabloids; an effigy of her body was found with a noose around its neck hanging outside a California home. And she was trashed in a sexist manner on nearly every news station across the country. Remarkably, she was given more respect and her views were treated more fairly by the British press in a nation where the Queen Mother has held high office for centuries.

As a former high school basketball athlete and star player, Palin understood that the game would be tough, but no one could have predicted that so many of the rules would be broken. Her resilience in the face of her adversaries was admirable; her fighting spirit held up until the end. She never lost her focus and her faith, her strength and her vision. Palin is a woman with an eye toward the future. She maintains her cool under pressure, deliberates, and does not react but waits to respond: admirable qualities all in a national leader.

As a woman of the last great frontier, Palin overcame in her own way the challenges presented to her. Her experience in local and statewide politics was far greater than most people were aware. Her popularity ratings as both mayor and governor of Alaska far surpassed the norm. And her public speeches were electrifying; even those who did not agree with all of her views found themselves inspired to participate in creating a better, stronger America.

Palin's education and professional experience in actuality exceeded Abraham Lincoln's before his presidency. He received only 18 months of formal education and was basically self-taught. And while a large, strong man, Lincoln avoided hunting and fishing on principle because he did not like killing animals. Palin, a petite woman, capable of killing and dressing caribou, was comfortable with the hunt and commercial fishing. In the political arena, she chose nationalism and offshore drilling to keep America independent from foreign oil, even at the expense of the Alaskan bear, an animal that some consider an endangered species. In Alaska, survival of the fittest reigns, and Palin's approach was to choose our national security over the security of some forms of wildlife. This was her heritage. She was raised as a frontierswoman with Christian values that carried over into her political views. And whether voters were in agreement or disagreement with her stance on many pressing issues, Sarah Palin never wavered from her basic beliefs throughout a brutal and trying campaign. She returned home to complete the work she had started as governor and which she had managed to continue while on the campaign trail.

With the support of her loving family and many friends, Palin will continue to be an inspiration to women who aspire to the higher levels of government office and to all women climbing career ladders to success. And like Abraham Lincoln, she has opened a window into a freer America for all, becoming as it were an elevated symbol of American democracy. Many are convinced that we have not heard the last of Sarah Palin on the national political scene.

TIMELINE: EVENTS IN THE LIFE OF SARAH PALIN

February 11, 1964	Born Sarah Louise Heath in Sandpoint, Idaho, to Sally and Chuck Heath. Family relocates to Skagway, Alaska.
1969	Family moves to Anchorage, Alaska.
1971	Family settles in Wasilla, Alaska.
1976	Receives baptism in the Wasilla Baptist Church.
1982	Plays on the Wasilla High School state championship basketball team. Graduates from Wasilla High School.
1984	Wins Miss Wasilla Beauty Pageant.
1987	Receives bachelor's degree from University of Idaho.
August 29, 1988	Elopes with Todd Palin and marries in Palmer, Alaska.
1989	First child, Track Palin, is born.
1990	First daughter, Bristol Palin, is born.
1992	Wins a seat on the Wasilla City Council.
1994	Second daughter, Willow Palin, is born.

1996	Inaugurated as mayor of Wasilla.
2001	Third daughter, Piper Indy, is born.
2003–4	Appointed to the Alaska Oil and Gas Conservation Commission (AOGCC).
2004	Runs for lieutenant governor but is not elected.
2006	Inaugurated as governor of the State of Alaska.
2008	Second son, Trig, is born. Runs on the Republican ticket for vice president along with John McCain for president; the ticket loses to Democrats Barack Obama and Joseph Biden in the November 4 election.
July 4, 2009	Announces her resignation as governor; leaves office at the end of the month.
November 2009	Palin's autobiography, *Going Rogue: An American Life*, is published.
2010	Joins Fox News as a political commentator and analyst.

Chapter 1

THE BUNNY TRAIL

Born to parents who would work for the federal government in their retirement, bravely assisting rescue workers at Ground Zero by keeping rats away from the remains of the victims of 9/11, Sarah Palin was destined to play a significant role in women's attempts to break the political glass ceiling, entering into the race for one of the highest offices in the United States, the vice presidency. Only three other women in American history had attempted election to the upper echelons of the national political arena: Victoria Woodhull, who ran for the presidency in 1872, along with Frederick Douglass, the former slave and active abolitionist, for vice president; Shirley Chisholm, the first black American woman to campaign for the Democratic presidential nomination in 1972; and Geraldine Ferraro, the Democratic candidate for vice president in 1984, running alongside Walter Mondale.

These women faced major political obstacles: Woodhull, a suffragist, was running on the ticket of the Equal Rights Party, which was considered outside the mainstream; Chisholm ran a grassroots campaign with very little funding and was unable to secure nomination; and Ferraro, the first female candidate running for a major political party, lost along with Mondale to the Republican duo of Ronald Reagan and George H. W.

Bush after Ferraro's husband's financial records had been subjected to close scrutiny in an attempt to discredit her. Sarah Palin would become the fourth woman in American history to run a campaign that had the potential of reaching the White House, but she would encounter many challenges along the way.

On February 11, 1964, Sarah Louise Heath was born to Chuck and Sally Heath in Sandpoint, Idaho, near the sandy shores of Lake Pend Oreille, only three months after the assassination of President John F. Kennedy. Sandpoint is noted for its magnificent sunsets, water sports, and panoramic vistas of majestic purple mountains surrounding the lake. Home prices in Sandpoint remain half the national average to date, yet it is one of the most beautiful scenic areas in the United States.

A month after Sarah Heath's birth, the powerful earthquake of March 27, 1964, occurred on Prince William Sound, Alaska. It was registered initially as 8.4 on the Richter scale, yet later it was reevaluated at 9.2, which made it the second largest earthquake ever recorded. Anchorage, while 120 kilometers from the epicenter, suffered the most damage of any city: 75 homes were sucked beneath the earth and disappeared. The J.C. Penney and the Four Seasons Apartment buildings were totally destroyed. The earthquake triggered giant tsunami waves 35 feet tall, and warnings of these waves were sent as far away as Hawaii and the Soviet Union. Within four minutes, 131 people in total were pronounced dead, 116 of them in Alaska and 16 in California and Oregon. Five thousand were left homeless.[1]

During this time, Sarah's parents moved the family to Alaska, where her father had obtained a teaching job in Skagway, "the point of embarkment for the famous Chilkook and White Pass Trails"[2] that had led gold prospectors to their destinations during the Klondike Gold Rush of 1897. Much of the town has been preserved, and hundreds of thousands of visitors arrive yearly to explore the shops and hotels that once provided food and shelter for the Stampeders (also known as Sourdoughs because of the yeast they brought with them to make sourdough bread), men who had come to seek their fortunes by panning nuggets out of the streams and lakes and by separating gold dust from the dense soil in the tall mountains of Alaska. The town of Skagway is relatively small even today, with one K–12 school, 13.5 teachers, a student-teacher ratio of 8:1, one chief of police, and three police officers.[3]

With three young children and a fourth on the way, Sarah's father, Chuck, worked for the school system while her mother, Sally, took care of her young family. Sally eventually took a job as a school secretary to help support the family. Sarah's youngest sister, Molly, was born shortly thereafter. All four of the Heath children were exposed to the wilds of the Alaskan terrain, where the temperature dips to an average of 16 degrees Fahrenheit in January. On the whole, however, temperatures in the Skagway area are relatively moderate compared with temperatures in the interior and northern areas of Alaska, which can range from zero to -20°F in winter (although rarely) to the 80°F to 85°F range nearly every year, chiefly in June, July, and August.[4] Sarah's father would take his family on outdoor expeditions, including fishing trips and journeys to the site of the Klondike Gold Rush to search for relics left behind by the Stampeders. In the days of the Gold Rush, the temperature in winter often went as low as 60 degrees below zero, an indication that global warming is affecting even the frozen terrain of Alaska. With such a cold climate as her home base, it is not surprising that, many years later, Sarah would choose to attend college for a brief time in the warm climate of Hawaii.

An undated family photograph against a backdrop of magnificent Alaskan scenery shows Sarah Heath (second from left) with her sisters Molly (left) and Heather and her brother Chuck. AP Photo/Heath Family.

As a child, Sarah became familiar with the independent, driven women who made their fortunes in the days of the Gold Rush, such as Annie Hall Strong, Nellie Cashman, Molly Walsh, Belinda Mulrooney, Klondike Kate, Harriet Pullen, and Ethel Berry, many of whom opened restaurants, supply shops, and hotels for the gold miners and provided much needed food and sundries in places along the trail of the Chilkoot Pass.

Forty thousand gold miners attempted the journey, but not all of them were capable of completing it because of the severe weather conditions and the difficult mountainous terrain. They were required by the government to take enough food and supplies for a year and were supervised by the Canadian Mounties in transporting these provisions 600 miles up the mountain from Skagway to the gold outposts, a most difficult task of which only the hardiest were capable. Each gold miner would need to take 50 round-trip treks up the mountain with his supplies in order to meet the requirements for a year-long stay, whether or not he intended to remain there so long.

The Canadian Mounties considered Skagway "little better than Hell on earth" during this time.[5] Some of the prospectors were too exhausted and disoriented to pan and dig for gold when they finally arrived. Many of the women, however, who provided goods and services, including food, shelter, and supplies, made huge fortunes in Skagway and along the route to the gold sites—unlike the majority of the prospectors.

One woman, Frances Dorley, became wealthy by cooking baked beans and baking bread, pies, and doughnuts for the men.[6] Another woman exhibited a remarkable pioneering spirit:

Another of the Yukon's early female entrepreneurs was a stocky blonde woman by the name of Mrs. Willis who set out from Tacoma, Washington, while her husband stayed home. Before the rush, Mrs. Willis operated a laundry and bakery in Circle City, which was the main mining centre in 1896. But when word of the Bonanza Creek strike reached Circle, she packed up her washboard, baking tins, and sewing machine and joined the exodus to Dawson, hauling her own 750-pound load by sled.[7]

While there were those who became millionaires overnight, the majority of the gold diggers came away with small handfuls of gold dust, and many squandered their money in the saloons and brothels that were developing along the trail and in the town.

It was here in the Klondike region that the culture of the Alaska natives intertwined with that of the adventurous Stampeders and the women who supported them. While there had been much friction between the Native Alaskans and whites in the area prior to the Gold Rush, by the height of the era, the Chilkoot and Chilkat peoples, who had formerly fiercely guarded the interior regions for hunting and fishing, now cooperated with the white prospectors who came in search of the gold to which the native Alaskans had previously paid little attention. These industrious indigenous peoples profited from the Gold Rush in their own ways: they worked as packers of the men's gear; they guided the prospectors along the trails and through the streams with which they were so familiar; and they hauled the prospectors' heavy gear over the mountains. These men were strong and able to carry loads of 200 pounds strapped to their backs, and their "women and children carried about 75 pounds each."[8] By the turn of the century, most of the natives were devout Christians and refused to work on Sundays, and thus the prospectors were forced to carry their own gear up the mountains at least one day of the week.[9] The Chilkoots and Chilkats also profited by making dugout canoes and skin boats made of moose hide. For increasing fees, these indigenous peoples would assist in carrying supplies, sometimes by boat, to the innermost areas of the mountains where gold could be found.

And while interracial sexual relations between Native Alaskans and white prospectors were practiced most casually (even while simultaneously frowned upon by many in the area), there were some men who went to live with native women in the forests. They were known as Squaw Men. George Carmack was indeed such a man: he had a common law marriage with a Tagish First Nation woman named Kate. Carmack had given up searching for gold and was spending his time fishing and wandering the interior regions of Alaska with the native Tagish people, when he and

two Tagish friends were salmon fishing on Rabbit Creek, a tributary of the Klondike River. As he habitually did, Carmack

occasionally stopped to swirl a bit of the river sand in his prospec-
tor's pan. He had seen a little gold, but nothing of particular note.
At day's end, the men made camp along the creek, and Carmack
said he spotted a thumb-sized nugget of gold jutting out from the
creek bank.

The two Tagish Indians later said that Carmack had been
napping that evening and one of them found the nugget while
washing a dishpan. Regardless, further investigation revealed gold
deposits "lying thick between the flaky slabs of rock like cheese
in a sandwich."[10]

It was this event that was said to have started the great Gold Rush of
1896.

The Klondike is also the region in which Sarah Palin spent the first
five years of her life. Its history has been preserved in the town, and
today it is a popular tourist area for visitors to Alaska. Tales of the brave
men and women who sought their fortunes in the cold and desolate
interior of Alaska would inspire Sarah's independent and adventurous
spirit, as would her parents' outings with the family into the wilderness.
In the forests surrounding Skagway, one might indeed come eye to eye
with a moose or a black or brown bear.

This is the also the place in which author Jack London joined thousands in search for riches and attempted to get ahead of the other
prospectors by taking a boat through dangerous rapids, eventually developing scurvy for lack of citrus fruits and proper supplies. Two of his
novels, *White Fang* and *The Call of the Wild*, feature sled dogs that brave
the wilds of the Alaskan interior and fight for survival.

The Heath family moved briefly to Anchorage in 1969 and then
spent two years in Eagle River, where one can watch salmon swimming up close near the Eagle River Nature Center. This area is an idyl-
lic mountainous landscape where black and brown bear, moose, Dall
sheep, mountain goats, and marmots reside amidst the tall mountains
and crystalline lakes, especially Symphony Lake near the South Fork
of the river, positioned between high peaks of the Harmony Mountains.[11]

The Heaths eventually settled in Wasilla, originally named for
the Dena'ina chief Wasilla, and also known as Benteh, or "among
the lakes," because it is situated between Wasilla Lake and Lake

Lucille.[12] The town is 748.9 miles northwest of Skagway, nearly a 15-hour drive away, a town which is basically a long strip of scattered development along the Parks Highway. Founded in 1917 as a railroad halt, the town increased in size with the completion of the Parks Highway in the 1970s. Eventually, it became the center of commercial activity in the Mat-Su Borough. The Old Wasilla Townsite Park, the original Wasilla School, an old barn and blacksmith shop, a reconstructed bathhouse, many historic homes, and the Dorothy Page Museum, named for the woman who founded the Iditarod Trail Sled Dog Race, are of historical importance.

The town of Wasilla today was described somewhat differently in the British newspaper *The Sun:*

> Wasilla—whose population of 7,000...—is a colourful mix of prosperous oil workers, hunters and hard-grafting families 50 miles north east of Anchorage...The main street is lined timber yards, the ramshackle Mug-Shot Saloon—where prospectors once paid for beer with gold nuggets—and charmingly named shops, including Big Shot Taxidermy, Bunny Boots and Happy Hooker Tows.[13]

The town itself is similar to many small suburban cities in the United States: it has a massive highway with many mini-malls lining the roadway and is somewhat victim to suburban sprawl, but it is distinctive in that its Native culture mingles with the mainstream culture. Totem poles, which were once part of the traditional ceremonies of the Native Alaskans, can still be found and in some cases are still employed as such today.

The area was predominantly Native until white settlers arrived in the nearby town of Knik in 1915. They relocated to Wasilla in 1917 following the construction of the Alaska Railroad. Some of the residents of Knik actually dragged their houses behind them when they relocated to Wasilla to be closer to the many advantages that the railroad system could provide. Wasilla remained a relatively small town until the 1970s, when there was a possibility that the capital might be moved to Willow. Suddenly, the population doubled; it doubled again in 1980–1982.[14] Today, low real estate prices and the opportunity to be close to Anchorage without living in a big city is the draw that brings many young families to the area.

It was here that Sarah learned to ice fish and hunt caribou. As the third of the four children born to the Heaths, she was one of the smallest adventurers. She and her family hiked a 33-mile trail when she was 8 years old, and she killed her first rabbit at age 10.[15] As she got older she learned how to skin and carve up caribou. The family also went hunting for wild birds such as the rock ptarmigan, which is indigenous to Alaska. Her parents engaged in these activities as sport and to provide additional sustenance for their large family which relied chiefly on her father's teaching salary. Chuck Heath has stated that "we raised our family to be able to support ourselves—90 per cent of our meat and fish we get ourselves."[16] Sarah was among the children who hiked the "bunny trail," a road which ran along the backyards of the houses in the neighborhood.

Their house was a small frame structure heated only by a wood-burning stove, and the stuffed heads of wild animals lined the walls. It has been described as "a cross between a natural history museum, science class, tackle shop and favorite grandparents' house."[17] On the lower level of their home, skulls may be found piled up on tables, antlers line the shelves, and photographs of people holding gargantuan fish are displayed on the walls. A photo of Sarah as a young girl running in the snow may also be seen.[18]

A family snapshot of Sarah Heath as a child in Wasilla. AP Photo/Heath Family.

With four children in their home, Sarah grew up learning to compete and cooperate, and she received unwavering support from her parents. Her mother's faith in God and her father's emphasis on sports and teamwork were among the values that would shape the woman she would become. Sarah shared a room with her two sisters, Molly and Heather, and they were very close throughout her childhood.

While Sarah was christened in the Catholic Church, she was raised along with her siblings in the Wasilla Assembly of God, a Protestant Pentecostal church that is unlike some of the energetic evangelical churches in the southern United States in that the sermons here are presented in lecture format rather than as impassioned speeches. According to Sarah Palin's biographer Kaylene Johnson, Sally Heath believed that she had found a "more meaningful path to faith"[19] in the Assembly of God congregation.

One of the beliefs of the Assembly of God church is that every individual should have a personal relationship with God. Some members of the Wasilla Assembly of God have engaged in the practice of speaking in tongues, although Sarah did not necessarily participate.[20] And while the church is a Pentecostal denomination, and the influences of its history have shaped the moral and religious fiber of Sarah Palin, she has repeatedly declared that she has never ascribed to a particular denomination but is a firm believer in Christianity and the Bible.

The Pentecostal movement, out of which the Assembly of God developed, originated in Prussia in 1817, migrated to Germany, and crossed the ocean with waves of German immigrants, taking root in the United States with the Azusa Street Revival in San Francisco, California, in the 1860s. As the churches spread out through the United States, a variety of different interpretations developed, and thus not every Pentecostal church espouses exactly the same beliefs.

The Wasilla Assembly of God's founding pastor, Paul Riley, who began his tenure there in 1951 and since his retirement in 1995 has worked as a prison pastor, was Sarah Palin's guiding spiritual beacon throughout the years of her childhood and up until 2002, when she changed churches to attend the Wasilla Bible Church with her own family.

Pastor Riley, while he believes that Sarah has deep faith, has refused to comment upon her spiritual journey. He believes that she switched to the Wasilla Bible Church because she has a large family and there were more children in attendance at Wasilla Bible. His wife, Helen Riley, has said, "My husband teaches the Word....It is preaching the Word as it is. It is not something for anyone's private interpretation. It is not for anyone to add to it or to take anything away."[21] To show her appreciation for Reverend Riley's guidance, as governor, Sarah Palin renamed a street near the church Riley Avenue.

According to Pastor Larry Kroon of Palin's more recent house of worship, the Wasilla Bible Church, "There are five core commitments we teach here, and that is the framework in which we try to live ... [:] the centrality of Christ, the authority of scripture, the priority of prayer, authenticity in our spiritual life, and community in our congregational life."[22] As a child, Sarah and her natal family often attended church frequently, on Wednesdays and twice on Sundays for morning and evening services. The Heath children also attended camps, Bible school during vacations, and other functions that brought them into community service, a major emphasis for practitioners of the faith in the Assembly of God church.

According to Pentecostal beliefs, baptism is an empowering experience which strengthens the faith and commitment of the person being baptized. And indeed, when Sarah was 12 years old, she chose baptism by immersion in the chilly waters of Beaver Lake. Sarah's sisters and mother joined her and were also baptized on the same day.[23]

Sarah's father, Chuck Heath, also played a great role in influencing her early years. As a science teacher in the Wasilla school system, he was very interested in the physical sciences and the Alaskan terrain. He also emphasized outdoor sports with his children, and during the year, he ran cross-country and track teams for his students and encouraged his own children to participate on various school teams. He ran in many marathons himself, including the Boston Marathon. During summer vacations, the television set was turned off. He set up a basketball hoop in their backyard. The children were encouraged to practice shooting hoops and to accompany Chuck on his many fishing, hiking, and hunting adventures. Competitiveness was encouraged, and Sarah, while not as gifted in sports as her brother, Chuck Jr., made up for skill with enthusiasm and determination to win. In recent years, she has transferred these qualities to the political arena, and she was determined to assist John McCain in the Republican campaign for the presidency. She worked by his side as well as independently in an effort to secure a win for the Republican team.

Alaska is a land of demanding climate, terrain, and natural resources, yet the people of this area have historically challenged the landscape as much as nature has taxed them. From early native Alaskans who survived this harsh terrain by hunting and fishing, to the Russian fur traders who ventured here in the late 18th century and eventually formed a fur company with America, to the sourdoughs of the Gold Rush in the late 1800s—and even those who today harvest fish and wildlife and harness natural resources such as oil and gas—the inhabitants of this land have been a strong, determined, motivated, and most importantly competitive people. They are hardy individuals who enjoy the great outdoors in one of the last natural wildlife frontiers in America.

Their energetic spirit has led them to establish competitions of strength and endurance such as the Iditarod Sled Dog Race and the snowmobile contest, the Iron Dog Race. Both of these demanding competitions test the ability of participants to master the landscape and climate of Alaska with both speed and endurance.

Although the Iditarod Sled Dog Races usually begin in Anchorage, the official headquarters of the Iditarod resides in Wasilla. Thus, when the dogs are running, they usually stop and restart in Wasilla, an event that brings most Alaskans into the great outdoors to watch and cheer on the men and women, known as mushers, who drive the sleds. The events begin in March, and they mark the end of the long, cold winter season.

The Iditarod Trail Sled Dog Race runs along the historic Iditarod Trail. The name may have several different derivations. According to Don Pitcher, *Iditarod* signifies "a path that had its origins in the 1908 discovery of gold along a river the Ingalik Natives called Hidedhod, meaning 'Distant Place.'"[24] Others have called it Haiditarod, suggesting that it was a trail originated by the Haida peoples, an indigenous tribe in Northern Canada and Alaska known for their artistic skill and their abilities as canoe and house builders and traders.

The Iditarod Races, depending upon one's perspective, commemorate one of two events in the history of Alaska: the purchase of the Alaskan territory—known as Seward's Folly, Seward's Ice Box, or Andrew Johnson's Polar Bear Garden—by the United States from Russia in 1867, or the events surrounding the 1925 diphtheria epidemic that gripped Nome, Alaska.

The town of Nome, which is across the Bering Sea from Siberia, gets only four hours of daylight in the winter. During the first few days of February in 1925, many adults and children in the area were suffering from diphtheria, and several people had died in Nome, which was cut off from air transport as a result of a blizzard raging across the vast Alaskan tundra. The engines of the planes froze as a result of the cold and blustery weather. The serum that worked to cure the disease was in short supply, but a large amount of it was located in Anchorage. It took 17 teams of sled dogs to transport the serum from Anchorage to Nome, a distance of 500 miles, and they completed the journey by relay in 5½ as opposed to the usual 10 or more days required for the trip. It was to become known as The Great Race to Mercy.

One of the drivers, Leonhard Seppala, along with his lead dog, Togo, took a shortcut over the ice, risking everything because Seppala's daughter was one of the children suffering from the disease. Once on solid ground, the ice behind him began to crack, and sections of it floated out to sea. Thus, the races that are run yearly from Anchorage to Nome are a family event that reflects the devotion of all the Alaskan people to their children and their willingness to battle the elements to save them.[25] Historically, the races have been conducted by both Native and white men. However, in 1985 Libby Riddles became the first woman to win the race. The Iditarod, which is also known as The Last Great Race, makes one stop on the trail, in Willow, which is very close to Wasilla. The teams restart the race in Wasilla as it is considered the headquarters of the Iditarod Dog Sled Races.

Indeed, competitiveness is a birthright in Alaska; only determined and persevering individuals could have initially settled in the beautiful yet challenging landscape. Beginning with the Native peoples who originally inhabited the land, to the prospectors of the Gold Rush, it has taken hardy individuals to compete with the climate and the terrain of Alaska.

Today, in the nearby town of Talkeetna, the tradition continues with the Mountain Mother Contest, a competition that requires mothers to perform a mixture of rugged outdoor activities including hunting moose, chopping wood, and hauling water as well as household tasks such as making pies, washing laundry, and changing diapers while carrying fake babies on their backs. And thus the competitive frontier spirit continues into the 21st century in the great northwestern state of Alaska.

Sarah Palin has harnessed this competitive drive and taken it to the national level in seeking the office of vice president of the United States while raising a family of five children. She has stepped out of the tundra onto the mainland to make her mark upon the national scene, and she is bringing all the energy, force, and determination of her native land along with her.

NOTES

1. *Alaska, a Documentary*, The History Channel, October 4, 2008.

2. Skagway Chamber of Commerce (1997–2002), http://www. skagwaychamber.org/community.html. Accessed on November 20, 2008.

3. Ibid.

4. Alaska Trekker, http://www.alaskatrekker.com/temperatures.htm. Accessed on November 22, 2008.

5. Schaller, David T., "Reinventing Skagway Schaller," http://www.eduweb.com/schaller/Skagway.html. Accessed on November 30, 2008.

6. White Pine Pictures, *A Scattering of Seeds: The Creation of Canada* [documentary television series], companion Web site, sidebar: "Women of the Klondike," http://www.whitepinepictures.com/seeds/ii/14/sidebar.html. Accessed on October 15, 2008.

7. Ibid.

8. Spotswood, Ken, "The Yukon Indians and the Gold Rush," *Klondike Weekly*, February 27, 1998, http://www.yukonalaska.com/klondike/indians.html. Accessed on October 16, 2008.

9. Ibid.

10. History.com, *Old West*, "This Day in History: August 16 1896, George Carmack discovers Klondike Gold," www.history.com/this...in.../george-carmack-discovers-klondike-gold. Accessed on October 24, 2008.

11. Swaney, Deanna, and Eric Amrine, *Eyewitness Travel Alaska*, ed. by Arundhti Bhanot (New York: Dorling Kindersly Publishing, 2006), p. 78.

12. Bell, Brian, ed., *Insight Guides Alaska*, 7th ed. (Long Island City, NY: Lagenscheidt Publishers, 2008), p. 217.

13. Smith, Emily, "I taught Sarah to shoot and butcher a moose… Washington won't scare her," *Sun*, Friday, September 15, 2008, www.thesun.co.uk/sol/homepage/news/the.../article1687959.ece. Accessed on October 3, 2008.

14. Pitcher, Don, *Moon Handbooks: Alaska*, 9th ed. (Emeryville, CA: Avalon Travel Publishing, 2007), p. 227.

15. Johnson, Kaylene, *Sarah: How a Hockey Mom Turned the Political Establishment Upside Down* (Carol Stream, IL: Tyndale House Publishers, 2008), p. 17.

16. Smith, Emily, "I taught Sarah to shoot and butcher a moose… Washington won't scare her," *The Sun*, Friday, September 15, 2008, www.thesun.co.uk/sol/homepage/news/the.../article1687959.ece. Accessed on October 3, 2008.

17. Davey, Monica, "Little Noticed College Student to Star Politician," *New York Times*, October 24, 2008, http://www.nytimes.com/2008/10/24/us/politics/24palin.html. Accessed on October 25, 2008.

18. Ibid.

19. Johnson, Kaylene, *Sarah: How a Hockey Mom Turned the Political Establishment Upside Down* (Carol Stream, IL: Tyndale House Publishers, 2008), p. 32.

20. Hilley, Joe, *Sarah Palin: A New Kind of Leader* (Grand Rapids, MI: Zondervan, 2008), p. 65.

21. Harper, Tim, "Media Probe Palin's Evangelical Views," *Toronto Star*, September 15, 2008, http://www.thestar.com/article/499314-Canada. Accessed on October 18, 2008.

22. Ibid.

23. Johnson, Kaylene, *Sarah: How a Hockey Mom Turned the Political Establishment Upside Down* (Carol Stream, IL: Tyndale House Publishers, 2008), p. 26.

24. Pitcher, Don, *Moon Handbooks: Alaska*, 9th ed. (Emeryville, CA: Avalon Travel Publishing, 2007), p. 228.

25. *Alaska, a Documentary*, The History Channel, October 4, 2008.

Chapter 2

NORTHERN LIGHTS

While Wasilla is a relatively small district in an arctic suburban frontier in the valley of the Chugach Mountain range located in the Matinuska-Susitna borough, the Wasilla community encourages all students to participate in sports, develop teamwork skills, and become competitive players.

As the Northern Lights, also known as the Aurora Borealis, light up the Alaskan skyline with an array of deep and ever changing colors during the long, cold winter months which provide only five hours of sunlight a day, so too did Sarah Palin bring light and color to her endeavors at Wasilla High School, brightening her own path and that of her classmates, especially in the area of sports.

Wasilla High School, which prides itself as "Home of the Warriors" and bears the slogan, "My Team, My Sports, Our World" has 12 categories of sports teams available to a student body of approximately 1,284, which far exceeds the usual number and variety of teams in small towns in the Lower 48. Among their mostly competitive sports are basketball, volleyball, football, soccer, baseball, track and field, cross country, skiing, swimming, cheerleading, wrestling, and "powderpuff," the girls' football team. In many of the team categories, there are different levels, such as Junior and Senior Varsity.[1]

Having acquired some of the skills of teamwork and cooperation with her three siblings at home, Sarah also developed a fighting spirit and competitive drive; she would now bring her energy and determination onto the track field and the basketball court, as well as in the classroom. Contrary to the "evidence" of a bogus report card that was posted on the Internet during her 2008 campaign for vice president, indicating that she was a poor student with a 2.2 grade point average and that her SAT scores were in the 400s in both English and math,[2] Palin was in actuality an honor student who worked as hard in the classroom as she did on the playing field.[3]

All four of the Heath children had participated in family games, hikes, and running and camping adventures. At home, they fought one another but made a pact to keep any injuries or damages secret from their parents.[4] Thus, there has always been a sense of pride and protectiveness among them. When Sarah scored the final points in the state championship basketball game, Heather waited for the phone call in her dorm at Washington State to find out if Sarah had won and to congratulate her. She said, "Boy, when they won, it was like I'd won too."[5]

Chuck Sr., helped coach Sarah on the track team at Wasilla High School. Approximately 10 years prior to Sarah's enrollment at Wasilla, her parents had taken up running, and Chuck Sr., who coached the track and cross-country teams, noted that his daughter's running ability became truly remarkable because of her determination and diligence: "In high school, she became my best distance runner." His laudatory statements in this regard are especially poignant since he did not consider that she had natural talent in sports.[6] Sarah's father later admitted that he was very demanding of the members of his team, even regarding his own daughter: "I just pushed her and pushed her.... My philosophy was no pain, no gain, and pay your dues, and the kid never argued with me."[7] Running has become a part of Sarah's life, and today she still runs frequently. Yet as an adult, Sarah prefers to run alone, which gives her time to clear her mind and work her muscles at the same time.

While Sarah was learning new sports in high school, she often woke up two hours before dawn to go moose hunting with her father. She learned to shoot a rifle and carve up caribou carcasses in the wee hours of the morning. Chuck Heath believed that his children should become independent individuals and learn how to fend for themselves in the land of the midnight sun. Chuck spoke to a reporter from the British newspaper the *Sun*: "Sarah was always very determined. Whatever she lacked in skill she always made up in determination. She always tried her hardest to be the best at everything she did ... she is a really good shot. I taught her to shoot a moose and dress it, to fish and hunt for game."[8] Although he always supported the family with teaching and coaching jobs and a variety of secondary jobs including working as a hunting and field guide and bartending to keep them financially stable,[9] Chuck has said that he and his wife raised the family to be self-supporting: "90 percent of our meat and fish we get ourselves."[10] Indeed, self-sufficiency is a hallmark of Alaskan culture.

During her nomination acceptance speech at the Republican National Convention, Sarah Palin introduced her parents, Sally and Chuck Heath. AP Photo/Charlie Neibergall.

While growing up, the Heath children were very close. The three girls shared a room that their father had added onto the house which was heated only by a wood stove. The girls brought in their own firewood but often just piled together on a bed to keep warm during the arctic winters. Her younger sister, Molly, sought Sarah's comfort by moving her bed closer to hers and holding her hand. Molly has said, "I was afraid of everything."[11]

Heather, her older sister who was a year ahead of her in school, explained that Sarah was an avid reader and had usually already read the books that she herself was assigned in class. Sarah also devoured newspapers end to end. As an adult, Heather Bruce remarked that "there was nothing really in high school that I would have thought would have directed her into politics except that she was probably a good debater at home."[12] Chuck Jr., her brother who is two years her senior, has commented upon Sarah's personality: "One of her strengths is being able to hold her tongue when she's been unfairly attacked. By staying true to her beliefs, things always seem to fall into place for her."[13]

While the Heath children had very different personalities, goals, and interests, they were all involved in sports of one kind or another. In addition to joining the track team, Sarah became a member of the basketball team in high school. While relatively petite compared with some of her teammates, she nevertheless made up for it in sheer willpower and focus. Initially she was not the most talented player on Coach Teeguarden's basketball team, yet he grew to respect her determination to improve. Nevertheless, he considered her to be a willful, independent girl. Sarah's determination, especially in basketball, earned her the humorous yet poignant title of Sarah Barracuda from her teammates. And like that deep-sea water fish, she would attempt to surprise her opponents and overrun them on the court, her eyes gleaming like a predator's in search of prey.

And pray she did indeed. Before major games, Sarah led her teammates in prayer. One morning as her coaches were wondering where the team had gone, they saw them walking toward them carrying Bibles in their hands.[14] Sarah often led the girls in prayer in a circle before the game was about to start as well. She truly believed in the power of prayer to assist her in all her endeavors, including those on the basketball court. She was the head of the school Fellowship of Christian

Athletes, and thus she took responsibility for leading the group in these religious activities.[15] Once, she even participated in an "ad-hoc church service on a particularly long ferry ride to a game."[16]

The Wasilla girls' and boys' teams often traveled together to play at various schools, and in this way Sarah became acquainted with Todd Palin, her future husband: "Like him, she proved to be a scrappy, tireless player. Never much of a scorer, she was brutal on defense."

By her junior year, she was eager to have more time on the court, and she attempted to persuade Cordell Randall, the assistant coach, to convince Coach Teeguarden to let her play more often.[17] As the Wasilla Warriors were entering into serious competition with the teams of much larger high schools in Anchorage, Assistant Coach Randall was determined that his junior varsity team, for which he was responsible, would become a winning team. He asked Teeguarden if Sarah and a few of her friends could play on the junior varsity team instead of the senior. Sarah wasn't pleased with this decision, but she played to the best of her ability and became a leader on the court among the younger girls. By the time she was a senior, she had earned the position of starting point guard and had become co-captain of the senior varsity team. By this time, Sarah had earned the respect and admiration of all her coaches.

Shortly before the state championship game in her senior year, Sarah sprained her ankle and was forced to wear a brace. She wanted to play in this important event for her high school, but she was benched throughout most of the game.

The final game in the playoffs was with Robert Service High School (named for the great poet of the Klondike, Robert W. Service). This was an Anchorage school with over 2,000 students. Because of her sprained ankle, Sarah was benched until the end of the fourth quarter. Then:

She played through the pain. The Warriors were leading in the dying seconds, but their opponents were fighting back. Sarah was fouled. She had the chance to clinch the game, and the state championship. 'Sarah Heath goes to the free throw line . . . the Warriors are ten seconds away from the 1982 state championship!' Coolly, she made the throw. 'Sarah's shot is in there! Sarah just aced the game for the Wasilla Warriors!' And seconds later, it was official. They'd won the 1982 state championship![18]

It was Sarah's free throw that won the game for Wasilla in the last 10 seconds of the game. Her teammates surrounded and supported her before she took the shot, while she made the shot, and after she won the game for the Wasilla Warriors. She told a reporter from the *Anchorage Daily News*, "I know this sounds hokey," she told the *Anchorage Daily News* years later, "but basketball was a life-changing experience for me. It's all about setting a goal, about discipline, teamwork and then success."[19]

Sarah's energy and interest in playing sports seems to have dimmed during her college years. Sarah was a young girl searching to find her way as an adult, but it appears that she never really found a college where she could excel as she had done in high school. She apparently "went from hometown stardom to college obscurity" as many college freshmen do; however, during the course of their education, most students find their niche, develop their special talents, and sometimes make life-long friends from other parts of the country. This was not the case for Sarah. There is no record of her ever having played competitive sports during the five years she spent earning her bachelor's degree between 1983 and 1987. And there is no indication that she participated in any of the campus extracurricular activities. Indeed, Roy Atwood, the adviser who was assigned to her at University of Idaho remarked that "I don't think she was terribly connected."[20] At the four or five schools in three states she attended during that time period, there is also no evidence that she wrote for any of the college newspapers or worked for a university television station, which might be expected of a student who was planning to major in journalism.

There are several possible explanations for this. Sarah had to pay her own tuition for college, as did all her siblings, and between jobs and relocating to find a school that would meet her needs, there appears to have been little time for outside activities. She may have been uninterested in socializing excessively, since her boyfriend, Todd Palin, remained back home to help with his family's fishing business, and she looked forward to spending summers working with him on his schooner. Perhaps she needed a respite from all of the intense competition which she thrust upon herself during high school. Whatever the reason, very few of Sarah's professors even remember having her in class, and several of her classmates whom she considered to be good friends also had a hard time placing her. This anonymity may have been the result of her transferring so often during the course of her college career.

The Heath family could not afford to make the rounds of college tours during summer, spring, and winter breaks for each of their four children, as many students and their families do in search of a college that is a good match. Consequently, she transferred five times before receiving her degree from Idaho State University at Moscow, her father's alma mater, with a major in journalism and a minor in political science in 1987. Yet exploring different campuses in warmer climates was considered to be quite the norm for students from Alaska venturing beyond the borders of their state, and her parents did not consider it out of the ordinary to transfer so many times. "'I went to 10 [colleges],' said Mr. Heath, who added that he and his wife did not provide their children's college tuitions; student loans did."[21]

Initially, upon graduating from high school, Sarah and three of her friends decided to take a break from the icy winters of Alaska and enroll at the University of Hawaii at Hilo. Before the semester was out, two of them had already returned home, but Sarah and her good friend Meg Ketchum, known to friends as Tilly, decided to remain in Hawaii. Sarah and Tilly enrolled at Hilo but never attended classes; instead, they transferred to Hawaii Pacific University in Honolulu where they took classes for only one semester. The girls had selected the school at Hilo from "pictures in a brochure,"[22] which didn't really give them much information about the college and its environment. Hilo was in a rainy area of the island of Hawaii and didn't provide the respite from harsh weather they were seeking. At Hawaii Pacific University, they took an apartment on the beach where they could study by the shore and learn to surf. Sarah was enrolled as a business administration student. By the end of this semester, they began to miss the cold weather and wanted to experience dorm life. So Sarah and Tilly transferred once again, to a small private liberal arts school, North Idaho College, which was situated near the shore of Lake Coeur d'Alene in the same lake country of Idaho where Sarah had been born. Her brother, Chuck, Jr., had gone to North Idaho College before transferring to the University of Idaho at Moscow. North Idaho was a very small, supportive liberal arts college, and the girls felt very sheltered there.[23]

At this time, Chuck was playing running back for the University of Idaho Vandals; he was the only one of the four Heath children to play NCAA sports. Unfortunately, he suffered shoulder injuries, which eventually prevented him from continuing his athletic career. Before he was injured and after she transferred once again to the University of Idaho, Sarah attended the games and cheered him on. She also decided upon majoring in journalism with a minor in political science. Her habit of reading newspapers over the years may have influenced this decision.

According to a fellow student at the university, Sarah once again became just an ordinary college student, "swapping clothes and going to parties. She drank..., but not much."[24] Sarah remained at the University of Idaho for five semesters, the longest she had stayed at any of the colleges she attended, only once taking a leave of absence for one semester to attend a local college at home to save money. However, she eventually earned her degree at the University of Idaho.

Sarah was considered to be a serious-minded girl interested in politics and the world around her. Several fellow students acknowledged that she was very quiet during this time and was uninterested in calling attention to herself. A friend who lived in her dorm, Stacia Crocker Hagerty, recalls that Sarah was "a calming presence" and "rock solid," and that Sarah had offered to pray for her when she was having boyfriend troubles.[25] This description of Sarah is interesting because Sally Heath, her mother, is considered to be "a quieter influence" and "the rock of the family" by friends.[26] Thus, during her college years, Sarah appears to have taken on some of the more reserved characteristics of her mother as opposed to the more aggressive and outgoing influences of her father. And while Sarah was attending a school that was considered to be a "party school" since the drinking age was only 19 until the year of her graduation, apparently the only prank that she played during her college career was pulling a fire alarm in the dormitory at the university. Her hands became covered with the dye that was released when she pulled the lever, and Sarah said, "Oh my God, look!" She admitted what she had done to the dean.[27]

While there are many indications that Sarah was a late bloomer regarding a focused career direction in her life, she may also have been rather homesick at college. Her roommate at University of Idaho, Ana de la Cueva, regarded her as "an easygoing person who loved to dance, took care each day with her hair and makeup, and would sometimes gaze out their window, missing Alaska's sunsets."[28]

Sarah's spirituality and interest in family life was important to her as a student, as may be indicated by her taking Religious Studies 133, which was described in the catalogue as "religious viewpoints as they relate to dating, courtship, and family life."[29] In addition to her many classes in journalism and political science, Sarah found time to wake up her classmates in time to attend Sunday services in the chapel.

While Tilly, her good friend from Wasilla, was intimidated by being required to videotape a 30-minute speech in front of a camera for a journalism class at North Idaho, Sarah was quite confident in preparing her presentation.[30] The fact that the class would critique her performance did not appear to cause her any distress, either. Her poise and ability in reporting the news eventually led her to land her first job after college as a sportscaster for KTUU Anchorage, an NBC affiliate.

During summers and on winter and spring vacations, Sarah earned her tuition by taking on a variety of jobs. She worked in an Italian restaurant and a seafood cannery, and most important, she fished with Todd Palin for salmon on his schooner. She also entered beauty contests in an attempt to earn money for college tuition. In her 2008 race for the vice presidency, on the Road to Victory campaign trail, Sarah would later use the theme song from the Miss America beauty pageant, "Isn't She Beautiful, Isn't She Lovely," as her own theme song preceding her entrance to the podium during campaign speeches.

Before returning to college in 1984, Sarah decided to enter the first of three beauty contests in which she would compete. Sarah's brother found it out of character for his sister to participate in pageants, and he teased her about it. None of the Heath children were given a free pass to college, and they all earned and/or borrowed their tuition. Many years later, during Sarah's vice presidential campaign, it was often misunderstood why she had attended so many schools. There were many blogs on the Internet questioning her so-called privileged experiences as a college student in Hawaii. Clearly, the facts prove otherwise. She was a working-class student seeking an education, and enrollment in various schools parallels the opportunities given to middle-class students to travel and visit schools before attending. While it may have been a mind-broadening experience, attending many colleges to get her degree did not afford her the opportunity to truly settle in anywhere. Therefore, it is not surprising that so few of her professors and many students do not remember her.

Beauty contests were only one of many of her part-time jobs as a student. When Sarah entered the Miss Wasilla contest, she was as focused on the goal as she had been on the basketball court, and she won. She went on to the statewide competition for Miss Alaska and came in third place (also known as second runner-up), and was named "Miss Congeniality" by the judges.

She seemed to enjoy the beauty pageant scene except for the fact that the judges made the contestants turn around when they were in their swimsuits so that they could get a better view of their derrieres. Her mother remarked that she had found the swimsuit competition "painful."[31] Sarah, nevertheless, walked away with her college tuition.

Although Sarah was popular with the contestants in the competition, the first-place winner, Maryline Blackburn, who was the first African American to enter the Miss America Pageant and who is currently a professional singer in Georgia, noticed her competitive nature: "Oh my god, she's gorgeous, she'll probably be the one who wins.... She had this look about her in her eyes that tells you she's calculating, figuring out 'How am I going to win this competition.'" Sarah later wrote to Blackburn at the end of the program: "I do love you. You're more admired than even you know. And please keep God Number One. He's got great things for you, baby. Love, Sarah Heath."[32] Sarah's competitive nature had appeared once again, and while she did not win first place, she earned considerable money for her tuition, approximately $1,000 to $1,200.

Sarah later entered a third competition, for Miss Big Lake, which is a town near Wasilla. Her sister Heather has indicated that she may have entered another competition in the area as well, but Sarah did not win any awards in these pageants. She may have been preparing for these contests by taking a body shaping class at the University of Idaho—or she may simply have enjoyed the exercise, since she had been used to so much physicality during her high school years.

Sarah was a remarkable young woman in that she could appear beautiful in an evening gown, charm the pageant staff and contestants into

Sarah Heath crowned as Miss Wasilla in 1984. Her prize money helped pay her college tuition. AP Photo/ Heath Family.

giving her the title of Miss Congeniality, and fearlessly make a news video of herself to be scrutinized by her classmates, yet she could also haul fish from the icy Alaskan waters on her high school sweetheart's fishing craft during summer vacations. The work on the commercial fishing boat that Todd's family owned was grueling. No matter what the weather, the fish must be brought in, and Sarah and Todd spent long hours roping in the Alaskan salmon. She was nauseated by the moving boat much of the time and found the job very difficult, but she persevered at it nonetheless. Several of Sarah's fingers were seriously injured (differing reports say they were broken or not broken) when another boat collided with Todd's. Nevertheless, she continued working the next day; she didn't want to disappoint her boyfriend.[33] In the fall of 1985 she took a semester off from Idaho and returned home to save money by attending Matanuska-Susitna College, a local community college, to further her education.

The fact that Sarah had switched colleges so many times did not seem to hinder her in any way, especially in her political career, a remarkable feat in an era when sticking with it no matter the circumstances was encouraged by the older generation, a generation which would stay with the same firm for 40 years and retire with a gold watch and chain. In actuality, her flexibility and willingness to move about frequently and adapt herself to new and ever-changing situations aided her greatly on the campaign trail in 2008. After graduation from college in 1987, she was eager to return home to her family, friends, and boyfriend, Todd Palin.

NOTES

1. Wasilla High School Web site, http://www.whs.matsuk12.us/. Accessed on November 10, 2009.

2. Denton, Nick, "Sarah Palin's High School Grades?" http://gawker.com/5061283/sarah-palins-high+school-grades. Accessed on November 15, 2009.

3. Radar Online LLC, http://www.radaronline.com/exclusives/2008/10/sarah-palins-report-card-indeed-a-fake. Accessed on October 27, 2008.

4. Johnson, Kaylene, *Sarah: How a Hockey Mom Turned the Political Establishment Upside Down* (Carol Stream, IL.: Tyndale House Publishers, 2008), p. 19.

5. Johnson, Kaylene, *Sarah: How a Hockey Mom Turned the Political Establishment Upside Down* (Carol Stream, IL: Tyndale House Publishers, 2008), p. 31.

6. Ibid, p. 27.

7. Davey, Monica, "Little-Noticed College Student to Star Politician," *New York Times*, October 24, 2008, www.nytimes.com/2008/10/24/us/politics/24palin.html. Accessed on October 25, 2008.

8. Smith, Emily, "I Taught Sarah to Shoot and Butcher a Moose . . . Washington Won't Scare Her," *Sun*, September 15, 2008, http://www.thesun.co.uk/sol/homepage/news/the_real_american_idol/article1687959.ece. Accessed on October 8, 2008.

9. Johnson, Kaylene, *Sarah: How a Hockey Mom Turned the Political Establishment Upside Down* (Carol Stream, IL: Tyndale House Publishers, 2008), p. 16.

10. Smith, Emily, "I Taught Sarah to Shoot and Butcher a Moose . . . Washington Won't Scare Her," *Sun*, September 15, 2008, http://www.

thesun.co.uk/sol/homepage/news/the_real_american_idol/article16
87959.ece. Accessed on October 8, 2008.

11. Johnson, Kaylene, *Sarah: How a Hockey Mom Turned the Political
Establishment Upside Down* (Carol Stream, IL: Tyndale House Publishers, 2008), p. 18.

12. Davey, Monica, "Little-Noticed College Student to Star Politician," *New York Times*, October 24, 2008, www.nytimes.com/2008/10/
24/us/politics/24palin.html. Accessed on October 25, 2008.

13. Johnson, Kaylene, *Sarah: How a Hockey Mom Turned the Political
Establishment Upside Down* (Carol Stream, IL: Tyndale House Publishers, 2008), p. 23.

14. Ibid., p. 28.

15. Benson, Kristina, *God, Prayer, and Sarah Palin* (Southfield, MI:
Equity Press, 2008), p. 145.

16. Davey, Monica, "Little-Noticed College Student to Star Politician," *New York Times*, October 24, 2008, www.nytimes.com/2008/10/
24/us/politics/24palin.html. Accessed on October 25, 2008.

17. Johnson, Kaylene, *Sarah: How a Hockey Mom Turned the Political
Establishment Upside Down* (Carol Stream, IL: Tyndale House Publishers, 2008), pp. 27–28.

18. *Inside Edition*, "Sarah Barracuda's 1982 State Championship,"
airdate September 4, 2008, http://www.insideedition.com/news.aspx?
storyID=2076. Accessed on October 23, 2008.

19. Davey, Monica, "Little-Noticed College Student to Star Politician," *New York Times*, October 24, 2008, www.nytimes.com/2008/10/
24/us/politics/24palin.html. Accessed on October 25, 2008.

20. Ibid.

21. Ibid.

22. Abcarian, Robin, "Sarah Palin's College Years Left No Lasting Impression," *Los Angeles Times*, October 21, 2008, http://www.
latimes.com/news/nationworld/nation/la-na-palincollege21–2008
oct21,0,2546859,full.story. Accessed on October 27, 2008.

23. Ibid.

24. Davey, Monica, "Little-Noticed College Student to Star Politician," *New York Times*, October 24, 2008, www.nytimes.com/2008/10/
24/us/politics/24palin.html. Accessed on October 25, 2008.

25. Abcarian, Robin, "Sarah Palin's College Years Left No Lasting Impression," *Los Angeles Times*, October 21, 2008, http://www.

latimes.com/news/nationworld/nation/la-na-palincollege21–2008 oct21,0,2546859,full.story. Accessed on October 26, 2008.

26. Davey, Monica, "Little-Noticed College Student to Star Politician," *New York Times*, October 24, 2008, www.nytimes.com/2008/10/24/us/politics/24palin.html. Accessed on October 25, 2008.

27. Abcarian, Robin, "Sarah Palin's College Years Left No Lasting Impression," *Los Angeles Times*, October 21, 2008, http://www.latimes.com/news/nationworld/nation/la-na-palincollege21–2008 oct21,0,2546859,full.story. Accessed on October 24, 2008.

28. Davey, Monica, "Little-Noticed College Student to Star Politician," *New York Times*, October 24, 2008, www.nytimes.com/2008/10/24/us/politics/24palin.html. Accessed on October 26, 2008.

29. Ibid.

30. Johnson, Kaylene, *Sarah: How a Hockey Mom Turned the Political Establishment Upside Down* (Carol Stream, IL: Tyndale House Publishers, 2008), p. 35.

31. Davey, Monica, "Little-Noticed College Student to Star Politician," *New York Times*, October 24, 2008, www.nytimes.com/2008/10/24/us/politics/24palin.html. Accessed on October 26, 2008.

32. Chapman, Dan, "Smyrna Woman Beat Palin in Pageant," *Atlanta Journal Constitution*, September 8, 2008. http://209.157.64.200/focus/news/2077556/posts. Accessed on October 23, 2008.

33. Johnson, Kaylene, *Sarah: How a Hockey Mom Turned the Political Establishment Upside Down* (Carol Stream, IL: Tyndale House Publishers, 2008), p. 38.

as, "The Iditarod is the biggie," "Purdue was killin' Michigan early on," "Chicago beat the Clippers bad," and, "he muscles it right back on the rebound." When she caught baseball manager Tommy Lasorda yawning in the dugout, she ironically commented, "He's gotta learn to relax," a witty phrase in context (but one she might have been directing towards herself during her sportscast).[4] She would later use colloquialisms and working-class slang in her vice presidential speeches as well to reach out to the masses, which had both positive and negative results depending upon her audience. In the video of her reporting sporting events, she commented upon the Port St. Lucie sprinkler system as it appeared on the screen watering the stadium grass as "sparing no expense to entertain the fans. They'll finally go off, section by section."[5]

In the videotapes of her work at KTUU, Sarah at times appeared more relaxed than one of the news station anchors. She did a fine job of presenting the local sports news, but when the male anchor asked her about the game that would be played the next day, she simply said, "They will play." The anchor replied, "Don't go overboard there, Sarah."[6]

Sarah was eventually paid as a substitute sports anchor and was becoming an excellent newscaster. Hernandez believed she would have a career in broadcasting beyond the local level.[7] However, seven months after her initial Super Bowl sportscast, Sarah Heath chose a different path and married Todd Palin, the man she had been dating since high school.

The town of Palmer is approximately 14 miles northeast of Wasilla, about a 20-minute drive along the scenic Palmer-Wasilla Highway. It was initially settled by farming families who took advantage of FDR's New Deal: "200 farming families from the relief rolls of northern Michigan, Minnesota, and Wisconsin...(were) shipped...here to colonize the Matanuska Valley." Today the town is home to Klondike Mike's Saloon and Sisters of Essence Holistic Center.[8] It was at Town Hall in Palmer that Sarah and Todd chose to take their wedding vows in a civil ceremony on August 29, 1988.

Their reason for choosing Palmer rather than marrying in Wasilla remains a mystery. On the 29th of August, which was a cool 58 degrees Fahrenheit, an average temperature for an Alaskan summer, they had intended to meet Sarah's sister Heather and her friends at a fair but decided to elope instead.[9] Yet according to state laws of Alaska, Sarah and Todd would have had to have applied for the marriage license at least three days prior to the 29th.[10]

Since they did not have witnesses with them for the ceremony, they reportedly canvassed two senior citizens from a state-run nursing home that was across the street from the courthouse. These elderly people, one in a walker and the other in a wheelchair, stood up for Sarah and Todd as best they could.[11] Todd placed on Sarah's finger a ring that she had purchased in Hawaii and that cost only $35. Sarah later commented about the ring: "I always thought, it's not what it's made of, it's what it represents."[12] Todd Palin explained the reason for their elopement: "We had a bad fishing year that year, so we didn't have any money.... So we decided to spend 35 bucks and go down to the courthouse."[13]

Dillingham, the town where Todd Palin was born and raised, is located in the Bristol Bay area and was at one time known as the "salmon fishing capital of the world." It is a small yet rapidly developing seaport town in which the local economy is supported by a few businesses that heavily rely on the fishing industry. Dillingham offers upward mobility to its citizens while maintaining the small-town characteristic of communication on a first-name basis.

The upper end of Bristol Bay experiences extremely strong winds and thus some of the highest tides in the world. Navigating the bay can be very difficult because in addition to the winds, there are a number of shoals, sandbars, and shallows.[14] This makes fishing for sockeye salmon, also known as red salmon, a daunting task for the traditional commercial fishermen of the area, one of whom is Todd Palin.

Over half the population of Dillingham is Native American. Todd Palin's Yup'ik Native Alaskan grandmother, Helena Andree, taught him traditional Native ways and instilled in him the value of hard work.[15] As a small child, Todd learned how to net and rope in the fish alongside his grandparents and eventually took over their commercial fishing business. He inherited his fishing license from his family as is common in the area. To some extent, the permit was granted originally because his maternal grandmother is part Yup'ik of the Curying tribe. Permits to fish in Bristol Bay are considered by all to be valuable assets. Todd continues to fish for Alaskan sockeye salmon here every spring, and his wife usually accompanies him.

Commercial fishing in the area has recently become less lucrative because of fish farms that have become popular. As reported in a Canadian Broadcasting Corporation program, fisheries researcher John Volpe at the University of Victoria, British Columbia, worries that overfishing and continuing the salmon farming industry without improving farming practices could lead to the collapse of the West Coast wild-salmon stocks. According to reporter Erica Johnson, "The vast majority of fish raised in Pacific net pens is actually Atlantic salmon, which grow faster and survive crowded net pens better." For the broadcast, Johnson explored the many problems with farming fish. The fish are given antibiotics, fed processed fishmeal and oils to enhance growth and thus become excessively fat for lack of exercise, and they are given additives to change their color from grey to pink, which is apparently necessary because their natural pink color disappears when they are kept in pens. Farms also endanger wild salmon: "The farms are trouble for the area's wild salmon which become covered in deadly sea lice when they swim under the giant pens" where the farmed salmon are crowded in huge nets.[16]

In a Fox News interview, Todd Palin spoke with journalist Greta Van Susteren about his commercial fishing experiences on the North Slope. The Palins have commercially fished together for many years, both before and after their marriage, and they arrange their schedules to be available during the four-week fishing season. Todd explained to Greta Van Susteren that the fishing season usually runs from approximately June 25 until July 1. He also gave a description of how he goes about catching the sockeye salmon: "Well, we use gill net. It's a limited entry permit that I purchased from my grandpa years ago, in the early '70s, where they—if you had enough points, then the state issued a limited entry permit. So there's only so many number of permits out there. And there's two different gear types where you drift out in the ocean with nets behind the boat, or you set net on the beach. You have the required space, and that's where you fish. So we set net."[17] In a good season Todd and Sarah Palin haul in 100,000 pounds of fish; however, the profits vary depending upon the price per pound that is being offered in a given year. Some years the Palins bring some of the fish home.[18]

In addition to working as a fisherman in Bristol Bay, Todd Palin has also worked for many years as a production operator, an engineer, and an executive for British Petroleum, commonly known as BP, an oil firm that conducts some of its worldwide business on the North Slope of Alaska. The company, which traces its history back to the Standard Oil Company of John D. Rockefeller, is a member of the consortium that owns the Alaska Pipeline, which transports oil from the North Slope south 1,200 miles to tankers in Valdez. The pipeline has been dubbed the "longest engineering project in American history." The engineers of the pipeline, which was completed and began transporting oil in 1977, took the environment into consideration: there are many above-ground stretches so that the oil does not melt the permafrost; there are also raised caribou crossings to ensure that migration habitats continue undisturbed.

Todd Palin has worked for BP on the North Slope since 1989, and he discussed the conditions under which he works in the Fox News interview: the temperature can go as low as "minus 80 below with some wind chill factor on top—with some wind on top of that.... We do some amazing things on the North Slope." Todd explained that it is important to "bundle up and you make sure that you know, you're going to be safe. And you always—you know, you really push safety, and if you start to get cold, you take a break and warm up." Todd also mentioned that the kinds of clothing required in such an environment involve new technology for warmth and protection. Yet when the weather is "terrible, when there's whiteout conditions where there's nobody running on the roads or anything and there's basically a stop-work on any outside activity...there is a limit to doing work outside."[19]

Todd likes what he considers to be a good job that has provided for his family for a long time. The work schedule on the North Slope is very untraditional as compared with the schedules of most other major corporations in the Lower 48. Todd works one week on and one off; some men work two and two. He also has an unconventional commute to work: "They have charter 727s that fly out of Anchorage to Prudhoe Bay, about an hour-and-a-half flight."[20] Todd and Sarah adjust their schedules further to include their commercial fishing endeavors in the summer.

Todd makes an excellent salary working for BP and by conducting his fishing operation, and the Palins as a couple make nearly five times the average income of families in Wasilla. In addition, "they

own a single-engine plane, two boats, two personal watercraft and a...
custom-built home on a lake that is worth three times the average of
other homes in town.... The couple also own four lakeside parcels, described in county records as 'recreation' sites. They encompass 35 acres
of forest along Trapper Creek near Safari Lake, north of Wasilla."[21]
They have worked very hard over the years to obtain the American
dream of financial success, respect from the community, and an upper-
middle-class lifestyle, yet they still consider themselves to be ordinary
working-class folk.

Clearly, the image of the average Joanne and Joe, the "hockey mom"
and the "First Dude," is the image that Sarah and Todd sought to project
as a couple during the 2008 presidential election campaign. While they
are currently in a very stable financial situation, the Palins started out
their married life quite differently, living with Sarah's sister Heather.
Later, they took a rental apartment for themselves.[22] During their first
year of marriage, they experienced many changes. Todd took the job
with BP, and Sarah became pregnant with their first child.

Alaskans tend to give their children unique names, and the Palins
are no exceptions. In 1989 Track Palin was born, the first of the couple's children. He was named after the track and field season. Bristol
was to follow in 1990, and she was named for Bristol Bay. Eventually
the couple had three more children: Willow, named after the state bird
of Alaska, the willow ptarmigan, who was born in 1995; Piper Indy,
born in 2001, who was named after the Piper Cub, a plane that Todd
owns and flies, and the Polaris Indy Snowmobile that Todd drove when
he won his first Iron Dog race; and finally, Trig Paxton, whose name de-
rives from a Norse word meaning "true" and "brave victory." Trig is also
a family name, in honor of Todd's great uncle, a Bristol Bay fisherman.
The name Paxton comes from the well-known snowmobiling area in
Alaska. Trig, their child with Down syndrome, arrived in 2007.

The children have grown up in a household with parents whose
schedules are rather different than the norm, yet they have adjusted
very well. Todd and Sarah are involved parents who take turns caring
for their family. When he is not working on the pipeline or hauling
fish, Todd has been known to cook meals, wash dishes, fold laundry,
and watch the children while Sarah is working in the state capital or is
on business trips.

Both parents, when not working, spend time and energy with their children, and sports is one of the activities in which they all participate. Sarah's parents, Sally and Chuck Heath, also help out with childcare for the working couple, even though the family employs a nanny. When Sarah first became governor of Alaska, she dismissed the chef who came along with the job and advertised the governor's jet on eBay, seeking to save the citizens of Alaska money.[23] (The jet was later sold to a Valdez businessman in a deal brokered by the Republican speaker of the Alaska House of Representatives.) In spite of their busy lives, both parents make time for their own special activities. Sarah runs to keep fit and enjoys fishing as a hobby, and Todd participates in Iron Dog snow machine races.

Snow machine is the name that Alaskans use instead of *snowmobile*, simply because they are used for basic transportation during the long cold winters.[24] They are not really considered recreational vehicles, except when they are used in the Iron Dog competition. Todd Palin is a champion in this arena: he is a four-time winner of the Tesoro Iron Dog, a 2,000-mile snowmobile race.

Only the hardiest Alaskans participate in the Tesoro Iron Dog Race, an intense competition of speed, skill, and endurance. The drivers follow one of the same paths as the Mushers in the Iditarod, yet they drive machines instead of running dogs. While there has been criticism by animal rights groups regarding cruelty and the death of some dogs in the Iditarod, Iron Dog races have perils of their own: snow machines can easily break down or malfunction in the extreme cold of the Alaskan tundra.

Todd makes time in his busy schedule for the intense preparation that goes into succeeding out on the ice and snow. "He's a "true Alaskan," proclaimed a Wasilla café owner.[25] Sarah is always by his side at the end of the race, waving the checkered flag and celebrating his finish.

According to the official Tesoro Iron Dog race description, "This is a team race, consisting of two (2) persons and two (2) snowmobiles (track driven and ski steered). The Trail Class teams may include two (2) or more persons, but each person must have their own snowmobile. The Pro Race Class for 2009 runs from Wasilla area, to Nome and then finishes in Fairbanks. The routing may be changed at the discretion

*Sarah Palin rides behind her husband Todd to the Big Lake, Alaska, starting line
for the February 2007 Iron Dog race. AP Photo/Al Grillo, File.*

of the board. The routes for Trail, Semi-Pro, and Masters Class teams
will be determined on a year-to-year basis. All participants will dis-
play honor and integrity throughout all of their involvement with the
race. These participants will brave subzero cold, bad visibility, and deep
snow to push their snowmobiles and bodies to the limits to reach the
finish line."[26]

Held annually, the Iron Dog race begins in Big Lake, with stops in
Nome and Tanana before ending in Fairbanks. Two-man teams race
snowmobiles that exceed well over 95 miles per hour in weather that
often hits -60 degrees. The grueling race requires at least five layovers
for a total of at least 46 hours to allow riders to eat and sleep. Even
though he suffered an accident in 2008, Todd Palin registered to race
in February 2009 and finished in sixth place.

The accident in 2008 was serious, yet Todd survived with only minor injuries. Some 400 miles from the finish line, he hit a snow-covered barrel
that sent him flying from his machine. He broke his arm—nevertheless,
with his teammate, finished the race in fourth place: "A race checker

at Galena reported that Todd hit the barrel and was catapulted into the air. "He flew about 70 feet off the machine." Todd was "likely protected from serious injury by Iron Dog rules that require competitors to wear not only helmets but body armor as well."[27] Thus the races can be extremely dangerous even for seasoned champions such as Todd Palin.

Todd Palin has been called a "moose hunter, oil worker, snowmobile racer and hockey fan."[28] In her address accepting the 2008 Republican vice presidential nomination, Sarah Palin described her husband concisely: "Todd is a story all by himself. He's a lifelong commercial fisherman...a production operator in the oil fields of Alaska's North Slope...a proud member of the United Steel Workers Union...and world champion snow machine racer." (See complete "Address of the Vice-Presidential Nominee" in appendix A.) She is very proud of all he has accomplished, and he has done extremely well for himself considering he has achieved success in so many areas of his life without the benefit of a college education.

Todd himself is proud of what he has achieved and grateful to his company, BP, for providing him with training and the experience he has gained from working on the North Slope: "For those of us who learn by touching and tearing stuff apart and for those who don't have the financial background to go to college, just being a product of that on-the-job training is really important."[29]

NOTES

1. *Mat-Su Frontiersman*, "We Know Sarah Palin," Saturday, August 30, 2008, 8:46 P.M. AKDT, http://frontiersman.com/articles/2008/09/06/opinion/editorials/doc48ba20a98c56e204165664.txt. Accessed on October 26, 2008.

2. Ibid.

3. Clarke, Norm, "Former TV Boss Remembers Palin," *Las Vegas Review-Journal*, September 13, 2008, http://www.lvrj.com/news/28344599.html?numComments=16. Accessed on October 27, 2008.

4. Republican VP candidate Sarah Palin's sportscast video, http://www.youtube.com/watch?v=WehZBADtyjw. Accessed on November 2, 2008.

5. Ibid.

6. Ibid.

7. Clarke, Norm, "Former TV Boss Remembers Palin," *Las Vegas Review-Journal*, September 13, 2008, http://www.lvrj.com/news/2834 4599.html?numComments=16. Accessed on November 14, 2008.

8. Pitcher, Don, *Moon Handbooks: Alaska*, 9th ed. (Emeryville, CA: Avalon Travel Publishing, 2007), p. 220.

9. Johnson, Kaylene, *Sarah: How a Hockey Mom Turned the Political Establishment Upside Down* (Carol Stream, IL: Tyndale House Publishers, 2008), p. 39.

10. Alaska Marriage License Information, Laws, Requirements, http://www.weddingvendors.com/marriage-license-laws/united-states/ alaska/. Accessed on December 17, 2008.

11. Johnson, Kaylene, *Sarah: How a Hockey Mom Turned the Political Establishment Upside Down* (Carol Stream, IL: Tyndale House Publishers, 2008), p. 39.

12. Wangrin, Stacy, Mitch, and Mark, "Palin Says Expensive Clothing Not Her Property," Associated Press, seattletimes.nwsource.com/html/… /2008285792_appalin.html. Accessed on November 14, 2008.

13. Lee, Jeannette J., "Todd Palin Unique among Nations' 5 First Husbands," Associated Press/*Anchorage Daily News*, May 27, 2007, p. 3, http://palintology.com/2007/05/27/todd-palin-unique-among- nations-5-first-husbands/. Accessed on December 21, 2008.

14. Fishing & Hunting Guides Bristol Bay Directory, www.visit bristolbay.com. Accessed on December 24, 2008.

15. Johnson, Kaylene, *Sarah: How a Hockey Mom Turned the Political Establishment Upside Down* (Carol Stream, IL: Tyndale House Publishers, 2008), p. 36.

16. Farm Raised Salmon, CBS News Broadcast: November 14, 2001, Reporter: Erica Johnson; Producer: George Prodanou, www.eurocbc. org/page252.html. Accessed on November 18, 2008.

17. Fox News Interview with Todd Palin, "Todd Palin 'On the Record,' Part 1," Greta Van Susteren, Tuesday, September 16, 2008, http:// buzz.yahoo.com/article/pub/http%253A%252F%252Fwww.foxnews. com%252Fstory%252F0%252C2933%252C423102%252C00.html. This is a rush transcript from "On the Record," September 15, 2008. This copy may not be in its final form and may be updated, http://www. foxnews.com/story/0,2933,423102,00.html. Accessed on November 17, 2008.

18. Ibid.

19. Ibid.

20. Ibid.

21. Seper, Jerry, "Palins' Finances Unusual for Alaskans," *Washington Times*, September 30, 2008, www.washingtontimes.com/news/2008/sep/30/wealth-makes-palins-no-ordinary-alaskans/. Accessed on November 23, 2008.

22. Johnson, Kaylene, *Sarah: How a Hockey Mom Turned the Political Establishment Upside Down* (Carol Stream, IL: Tyndale House Publishers, 2008), p. 39.

23. Kornblut, Anne E., "Plane Not Sold on EBay," *Washington Post*, September 5, 2008, http://voices.washingtonpost.com/44/2008/09/05/plane_not_sold_on_ebay.html. Accessed on November 18 2008.

24. Roberts, Roxanne, and Amy Argetsinger, "'Snowmobile'? That Doesn't Cut it in Alaska," *Washington Post*, Friday, October 24, 2008; p. C03, www.washingtonpost.com/wp-dyn/.../AR2008102302118.html. Accessed on November 15, 2008.

25. Café owner Ben Harrell, quoted in Miller, Marjorie, "Todd Palin, Husband of Sarah Palin: A 'True Alaskan,'" *Los Angeles Times*, September 7, 2008, www.latimes.com/news/politics/la-na-todd7–2008sep07,0,58. Accessed on October 23, 2008.

26. Tesoro Iron Dog Race, http://www.irondog.org/race_coverage/about.htm. Accessed on October 28, 2009.

27. Medred, Craig, "Todd Palin Crashes in Iron Dog," *Anchorage Daily News*, February 15, 2008, 2:09 P.M. Last modified: February 15, 2008, 3:30 P.M., www.adn.com/news/alaska/story/316352.html. Accessed on November 14, 2008.

28. Miller, Marjorie, "Todd Palin, Husband of Sarah Palin: A 'True Alaskan,'" *Los Angeles Times*, September 7, 2008, www.latimes.com/news/politics/la-na-todd7–2008sep07,0,58. Accessed on October 23, 2008.

29. Reed, Bruce, "What Won't You Do for Us Lately? The Next President Doesn't Have to Solve Everything at Once," *Slate.com*, October 7, 2008, http://www.slate.com/id/2199720. Accessed on August 26, 2010.

Chapter 4

VIEWS AND VALUES

On October 24, 2008, during her vice presidential campaign, Sarah Palin addressed an audience of supporters in Pittsburgh, Pennsylvania, many of whom were concerned with the issue of children with disabilities. In this campaign speech, she eloquently summarized her position on both abortion and special-needs children. She spoke about the value of the lives of these children and the importance of the manner in which we treat them: "And what's been confirmed in me is every child has something to contribute to the world, if we give them that chance. You know that there are the world's standards of perfection, and then there are God's, and these are the final measure. Every child is beautiful before God, and dear to Him for their own sake. And the truest measure of any society is how it treats those who are most vulnerable."[1] Her speech was well received by the audience, and many parents approached her at the conclusion of the rally.

It is often impossible to separate a person's views from his or her values, and Sarah Palin is a fine example of this idea in action. Although she identifies her religion simply as Christian and has attended the services of different denominations of the Christian faith as an adult, she was raised in a Pentecostal church, and values she learned as a young child have clearly influenced her current opinions. More importantly, they have had an impact on her political ideas. The values she learned as a child in her family while growing up in Alaska also contributed to her views on many issues relating to the role of the family as it intersects with politics and law. Her husband's part–Native Alaskan Yup'ik ethnicity has also played a role in the development of her attitudes about society and the governance of Alaska. All of these factors have influenced the development of her position regarding several important concerns of the day, including abortion, children with special needs, and gay marriage. Palin's strong stance on these matters has profoundly influenced many of her own choices in life and has also impacted upon the lives of those she has touched through her political decisions while in office.

Palin's position on abortion springs directly from her Christian beliefs, and she is without contention a "right-to-lifer." She asserts wholeheartedly that every child, no matter the circumstances of his or her birth, has a right to be born and given a chance to thrive. During her campaign for lieutenant governor of Alaska in 2002, she "sent an e-mail to the anti-abortion Alaska Right to Life Board saying she was as 'pro-life as any candidate can be' and claimed to have 'adamantly supported our cause since I first understood, as a child, the atrocity of abortion.'"[2]

Many people, even her supporters during her various political campaigns, do not agree with her on this issue because she takes the hard line that even if a woman or young girl is raped, the child should still have every opportunity to be born since life begins at conception. Her actions have supported her beliefs in that she chose to bring to term her fifth child, Trig, who was diagnosed with Down syndrome. On the campaign trail for the vice presidency in 2008, she repeatedly told supporters with special-needs children, "I'm gonna make sure that all these children and families know that they have a friend in the White House."[3]

There are those who agree with Palin's position on abortion simply from a religious perspective, and others believe that abortion in the United States has become an issue of eugenics: "Abortion rights supporters—who believe that a woman has the right to make decisions about her own body—have had to grapple with the reality that the

right to choose may well be used selectively to abort fetuses deemed ge-
netically undesirable. And many are finding that, while they support a
woman's right to have an abortion if she does not want to have a baby,
they are less comfortable when abortion is used by women who don't
want to have a particular baby."[4] The extreme logical development of
this idea is that mothers will soon be given the opportunity to select
the child they want to abort based not only upon medical health but
congenital defects, sports ability, and even eye and hair color: "The
questions may only become murkier if testing extends to traits like ho-
mosexuality or intelligence."[5] Even supporters of the continuation of
legalized abortion have some reservations about this especially controversial subject: " 'Some religious conservatives say that they trust God
to give them the child that is meant to be,' wrote Ann Althouse, a law
professor in Madison, Wisconsin, who identifies herself as an abortion
rights supporter... 'But isn't there something equivalent for social lib-
erals? Shouldn't they have moral standards about what reasons are ac-
ceptable for an abortion?' "[6] This adds a whole new dimension to the
abortion debate, but Sarah Palin's views on this subject remain unwavering. There is no instance, other than if the mother's life is at risk,
in which she would condone an abortion. In an interview with ABC
News correspondent Charlie Gibson, on September 12, 2008, Palin
stated that she believed *Roe v. Wade* should be overturned:

Gibson: *Roe v. Wade*, do you think it should be reversed?
Palin: I think it should and I think that states should be
          able to decide that issue....I am pro-life. I do respect
          other people's opinion on this, also, and I think that a
          culture of life is best for America....What I want to
          do, when elected vice president, with John McCain,
          hopefully, [will] be able to reach out and work with
          those who are on the other side of this issue, because
          I know that we can all agree on the need for and the
          desire for fewer abortions in America and greater sup-
          port for adoption, for other alternatives that women
          can and should be empowered to embrace, to allow
          that culture of life. That's my personal opinion on this,
          Charlie."[7]

Supporters of *Roe v. Wade* believe that a woman should have the right to make a choice. Prior to 1973, when the Supreme Court decided *Roe v. Wade,* abortion was considered to be a criminal act: "State criminal abortion laws, like those involved here, that except from criminality only a life-saving procedure on the mother's behalf without regard to the stage of her pregnancy and other interests involved violate the Due Process Clause of the Fourteenth Amendment, which protects against state action the right to privacy, including a woman's qualified right to terminate her pregnancy. Though the State cannot override that right, it has legitimate interests in protecting both the pregnant woman's health and the potentiality of human life, each of which interests grows and reaches a 'compelling' point at various stages of the woman's approach to term."[8]

Prior to the landmark decision of 1973, many women had resorted to illegal, "back-alley" abortions, which were often performed in unsanitary conditions and which frequently left them sterile or injured by doctors and those pretending to be doctors. According to the National Abortion Federation, "Many women died or suffered serious medical problems after attempting to self-induce their abortions or going to untrained practitioners who performed abortions with primitive methods or in unsanitary conditions. During this time, hospital emergency room staff treated thousands of women who either died or were suffering terrible effects of abortions provided without adequate skill and care."[9]

While the "assertion of rape was not a factor in the Supreme Court's ruling, which established a woman's constitutional right to an abortion,"[10] Norma McCorvey, the woman who used the name Jane Roe as a pseudonym to protect her privacy in the *Roe v. Wade* case, came forward in 1987 and admitted that her previous claim that she had been raped was a lie. Her reason for the deception was that she thought that if the Texas court thought she had been raped, it might be more sympathetic toward her: "Ms. McCorvey [stated] that she had fabricated her account of being raped by three men and a woman in 1969 because she had hoped to circumvent a 100-year-old Texas law that banned abortions except when the woman's life was in danger.... Ms. McCorvey was 21 years old when she became pregnant. At the time, she was working as a waitress and...was too poor to travel to California, the closest state where abortion was legal, or to afford local illegal abortionists."[11] McCorvey's attorney before the Supreme Court avoided mentioning the alleged rape altogether because of the larger social issue: "Sarah Weddington, one of the two lawyers who took the case to the Supreme Court, said she had never 'touched the issue of rape and only emphasized the question of whether the Constitution gives to the state or leaves to a woman the questions of what she can or must do with her body.'"[12]

The Roe v. Wade decision changed the social climate in America. Many women felt that it gave them power over their own bodies: "The Court's opinion decides that a State may impose virtually no restriction on the performance of abortions during the first trimester of pregnancy. Our previous decisions indicate that a necessary predicate for such an opinion is a plaintiff who was in her first trimester of pregnancy at some time during the pendency of her law-suit."[13] Norma McCorvey gave birth before the proceedings ended and chose to give up the child for adoption.

On January 22, 1973, Roe v. Wade passed into law. Consequently, the role of religion and morality became an issue in the political arena: "The Court today is correct in holding that the right asserted by Jane Roe is embraced within the personal liberty protected by the Due Process Clause of the Fourteenth Amendment....It is evident that the Texas abortion statute infringes that right directly. Indeed, it is difficult to imagine a more complete abridgment of a constitutional freedom than that worked by the inflexible criminal statute now in force in Texas. The question then becomes whether the state interests advanced to justify this abridgment can survive the 'particularly careful scrutiny' that the Fourteenth Amendment here requires."[14] This last statement was the loophole that would allow for future examination of the abortion laws.

The change in abortion laws through Roe v. Wade was a major victory for feminists in the early 1970s. The decision not only invalidated state laws, but it also influenced attitudes in America regarding the procedure. And while the decision confirmed the concern over women's health, it also validated the interest in protecting the unborn fetus.

Over the years, Sarah Palin's views on abortion have been reflected in her stance on relevant legislation: in October 2006, she opposed using federal funds for abortion, and in the same year, she indicated that if Roe v. Wade was overturned, the people should decide what to do next.[15] In October of 2008, she held the position that abortion should be state rather than federally regulated.

Another concern connected with the issue of legalized abortion is that problems sometimes arise during amniocentesis. The procedure itself can be risky for the mother and fetus, and in recent years, the results for certain types of diagnoses have proven to be inaccurate.

There are several methods for testing for spina bifida, including a simple blood test, amniocentesis, ultrasound, spinal X-rays, magnetic resonance imaging (MRI) scans, and computed tomography (CT) scans. These tests can also help to determine if the child has Down syndrome or a variety of other birth defects.

Some of the tests are simple to perform, and others are a bit more complicated and present possible risks. The "simple blood test...may also indicate fetal brain defects, multiple fetuses, a miscalculated due date or Down syndrome. Typically, AFP [alpha-fetoprotein] screening is performed by a woman's obstetrician. If test results are high, the test may be repeated to confirm. If test results still indicate a potential risk for spina bifida or other birth defects, patients may be referred...for follow-up testing. Ultrasound...may detect a spinal cord defect caused by spina bifida or discover other reasons for high levels of alpha-feto-protein (AFP)."[16]

Amniocentesis is performed between the 15th and 20th weeks of pregnancy. The test may be recommended to women who have high levels of AFP that cannot be explained by an ultrasound. Amniocentesis is also used in detecting the sex of the fetus before birth, and thus many women opt for the exam so that they can prepare for the arrival of a girl or boy—often without considering the risks of the test itself, which involves injecting a needle into the amniotic sac and extracting fluid for testing. This can and sometimes does bring about spontaneous abortion of the fetus: "The test is generally considered safe. It can lead to miscarriage in about 1 in 200 to 1 in 400 women. Amniocentesis is 99 percent accurate for detecting Down syndrome and about 90 percent accurate for detecting other chromosomal abnormalities and spina bifida."[17] With the possibility of inaccuracy in testing for birth defects, however, the notion that literally hundreds of thousands of women could be aborting normal or even exceptionally gifted children adds yet another dimension to the debate.

Among the many possible defects that can occur in vitro, spina bifida—an open or severed spine—is considered to be one of the most serious. Portions of the spinal column protrude, making them vulnerable to injury or infection. Recently there has been some controversy over the diagnosis of spina bifida in vitro because some children diagnosed with the disorder in vitro actually manifest intellectual giftedness when brought to term. Apparently, the genes for spina bifida and giftedness often resemble one another. Yet according to New York-Presbyterian Hospital, "Learning disabilities and developmental delays are common with spina bifida. In addition, long-term rehabilitation often is required after surgery. Babies with spina bifida also are at high risk of developing a latex allergy due to exposure to latex from multiple medical and surgical procedures."[18]

John McCain spoke of Sarah Palin's compassion for families with special-needs children during the 2008 campaign: most people assumed he was referring to her son Trig, her fifth child, who is a Down syndrome baby. He noted that she "understands special-needs families....

On a blustery October 18, 2008, Republican vice presidential nominee Sarah Palin addresses a rally in Lancaster, Pennsylvania. Courtesy of the author.

She understands that autism is on the rise, that we've got to find out what's causing it, and we've got to reach out to these families, and help them, and give them the help they need as they raise these very special needs children. She understands that better than almost any American that I know."[19] McCain was criticized by the press as well as by many individuals for this statement because it appeared that he might have confused Down syndrome with autism, but he was quite correct in stating that Palin is knowledgeable about the subject. She spoke of her sister and her sister's son, who is autistic, in her speech to an audience comprised of special-needs advocates and parents of children with disabilities in Pittsburgh, Pennsylvania, on October 24, 2008: "My best friend, who happens to be my sister, Heather...her 13-year old son Karcher...has autism. Heather and I have worked on this for over a decade. Heather is an advocate for children with autism in Alaska. And as governor, I've succeeded in securing additional funding and assistance for students with special needs. By 2011, I will have tripled the funding available to these students."[20]

Sarah Palin believes that the government should provide additional assistance and support services to families with special-needs children of any disability. Charlie Gibson queried Palin about exceptions to her position on abortion in the September 12, 2008, interview. Although she took a harder line than John McCain on the abortion issue, her "sentiments [were] 'personal opinion[s]' that could potentially differ from official policy in a McCain White House":

Gibson: John McCain would allow abortion in cases of rape
            and incest. Do you believe in it only in the case where
            the life of the mother is in danger?
Palin: That is my personal opinion.
Palin: My personal opinion is that abortion [should be] al-
            lowed if the life of the mother is endangered. Please un-
            derstand me on this. I do understand McCain's position
            on this. I do understand others who are very passionate
            about this issue who have a differing [opinion].[21]

Sarah Palin explained the decision that she and Todd made regarding her own child with Down syndrome: "We've both been very vocal about being pro-life....We understand that every innocent life has wonderful potential."[22]

She outlined policy changes for children with disabilities. She summarized the three areas that would be improved if she and McCain were elected: more choices for parents in selecting appropriate education and special services; fully funding IDEA (Individuals with Disabilities Education Act), which had recently been experiencing funding cuts; and efforts to reform and refocus, including providing information and assistance to families of special needs infants and toddlers, increasing funding to states, and increasing services to high school and community college students by modernizing the Vocational Rehabilitation Act. According to a statement put out by the McCain-Palin Campaign, "Only 52 percent of students with disabilities graduate with a regular high school diploma, and 33 percent of students with disabilities drop out of the education system entirely. John McCain and Sarah Palin believe we can, and must, do better."[23]

Palin spoke passionately about the pride she takes in her son and in other children with special needs: "One of the most wonderful experiences in this campaign has been to see all the families of children with special needs who come out to rallies and events just like this. We have a bond there. We know that children with special needs inspire a special love. You bring your sons and daughters with you, because you are proud of them, as I am of my son."[24]

Palin also opposes stem cell research on embryos. She explicated her ideas regarding this controversial subject when speaking with Charlie Gibson:

Gibson: Embryonic stem cell research, John McCain has been supportive of it.

Palin: You know, when you're running for office, your life is an open book and you do owe it to Americans to talk about your personal opinion, which may end up being different than what the policy in an administration would be. My personal opinion is we should not create human life, create an embryo and then destroy it for research, if there are other options out there....And thankfully, again, not only are there other options, but

we're getting closer and closer to finding a tremendous
amount more of options, like, as I mentioned, the adult
stem cell research."[25]

During her first years of motherhood, Sarah Palin stayed home with
her oldest son, Track, and continued to do so for the first five years of
his life. Yet thereafter, while raising him and her other small children,
she worked at several jobs to help support her young and growing family. She was fortunate to have an extended family of her own, including
her two parents, to participate in the care and rearing of her children.
She also has had the support of her husband's extended family, which
includes the children's great-grandmother of native Alaskan descent
who believes in helping to take care of everyone in the family and par-
ticipating in whatever jobs need to be done.

Sarah Palin never had to face a pregnancy alone without a supportive family around her as many young women do today as a result of
the deterioration of the American family. Her experience as part of a
society that has built-in familial networks and conservative, traditional
religious values is not the experience of many unwed mothers today.

On September 1, 2008, it was announced that the Palins' unmarried
eldest daughter, Bristol, was pregnant. According to the *Washington
Post*, Sarah Palin then "faced many critics who noted that as governor,
she significantly cut state aid for Covenant House Alaska, an agency
that serves at-risk youth and teen mothers.... Palin 'reduced funding
for Covenant House Alaska by more than 20 percent, cutting funds
from $5 million to $3.9 million.'"[26] Covenant House Alaska is a mix
of programs and shelters for troubled youths, including Passage House,
which is a transitional home for teenage mothers.

Dr. Warren Throckmorton, Professor of Psychology at Grove City
College in Pennsylvania and a Fellow for Psychology at the Center
for Values and Vision, conducted research into the figures used by the
Washington Post, and contradicted the *Post's* findings: "What is mis-
leading about the *Post* headline is that the allocation of 3.9 million is
three times more than Covenant House Alaska received from government grants in 2007. According to records on the Covenant House
Alaska website, the organization received just over 1.3 million dollars
from grants in 2007 and nearly 1.2 million in 2006. Even with the

reductions, Governor Palin signed a budget which provided three times more funds than the organization received in 2007."[27]

The *Anchorage Daily News* reported in August 2006 that Palin stated that "no woman should have to choose between her career, education and her child [and that] she is pro-contraception and said she's a member of a pro-woman but anti-abortion group called Feminists for Life."[28]

During the 2008 campaign, Palin requested that her daughter Bristol be left alone by the media. This has been the tradition for candidates' children in the past, and Palin hoped that the media would respect her wishes; for the most part, they did. At that time Bristol had plans to marry in the near future. Were it not for her loving family, Bristol would have faced the same challenges as the young women who are provided services by Passage House. This agency helps women in need find appropriate jobs and/or education so that they may better provide for their children.

Gay marriage is another issue concerning which Sarah Palin has strong convictions. Her beliefs on this subject stem from her religious background in churches that take a literal interpretation of the Bible. Palin has said that she is not judgmental and has good friends who are gay. Although she has opposed gay marriage based upon her biblical background, she "has often sympathized with the concerns of the gay community about discrimination and has implemented legislation ensuring equal benefits for same-sex couples."[29] Nevertheless, she supported the 1998 constitutional amendment which was passed 2 to 1 to ban gay marriage in Alaska, agreeing that the definition of marriage is the union of a man and a woman.

In an interview with David Brody in Lancaster, Pennsylvania, on October 20, 2008, Palin responded to Brody's questions about the gay marriage amendment, noting that the majority of people in her state agreed that it was necessary "to vote to amend the Constitution defining marriage as between one man and one woman" and that it is the right of individuals to defend traditional marriage as the "foundation of our society":

I wish on a federal level that that's where we would go because I don't support gay marriage. I'm not going to be out there judging individuals, sitting in a seat of judgment telling what they can and can't do, should and should not do, but I certainly can express my own opinion here and take actions that I believe would be best for traditional marriage.[30]

NOTES

1. "Remarks by Governor Sarah Palin on the McCain-Palin Commitment to Children with Special Needs," Arlington, Virginia— McCain-Palin Press Office, Friday, October 24, 2008.

2. Hopkins, Kyle, "Same-Sex Unions, Drugs Get Little Play," *Anchorage Daily News*, August 6, 2006, http://www.adn.com/news/politics/elections/governor06/story/183895.html. Accessed on November 20, 2008.

3. "Road to Victory" rally speech, Lancaster, Pennsylvania, October 18, 2008.

4. Harmon, Amy, "Genetic Testing + Abortion=???" *New York Times*, May 13, 2007, http://www.geneticsandsociety.org/article.php?id=3469. Accessed on November 19, 2008.

5. Ibid.

6. Ibid.

7. Goldman, Russell, "Sarah Palin Defends Abortion Stance, Explains 'Bridge to Nowhere' Support," Charles Gibson in exclusive interview, *ABC News Report*, September 12, 2008, http://abcnews.go.com/Politics/Vote2008/story?id=5787748&page=1. Accessed on November 20, 2008.

8. U.S. Supreme Court, *Roe v. Wade*, 410 U.S. 113 (1973) 410 U.S. 113 Roe et al. v. Wade, District Attorney of Dallas County Appeal from the United States District Court for the Northern District of Texas No. 70–18. Argued December 13, 1971. Reargued October 11, 1972. Decided January 22, 1973.

9. "History of Abortion," National Abortion Federation, NAF Web site, 2008, http://www.prochoice.org/about_abortion/history_abortion.html. Accessed on November 21, 2008.

10. Noble, Kenneth B., "Key Abortion Plaintiff Now Denies She Was Raped," *New York Times*, September 9, 1987, http://query.nytimes.com/gst/fullpage.html?res=9B0DE2DD113EF93AA3575AC0A961

948260&sec=&spon=&pagewanted=2. Accessed on November 22, 2008.

11. Ibid.

12. Ibid.

13. Ibid.

14. U.S. Supreme Court, *Roe v. Wade*, 410 U.S. 113 (1973) 410 U.S. 113 Roe et al. v. Wade, District Attorney of Dallas County Appeal from the United States District Court for the Northern District of Texas No. 70–18. Argued December 13, 1971. Reargued October 11, 1972. Decided January 22, 1973.

15. "Sarah Palin on Abortion," *Time*, http://www.time.com/time/specials/packages/article/0,28804,1849557_1849562_1849823,00.html. Accessed on November 22, 2008.

16. Spina bifida, http://www.ucsfhealth.org/childrens/medical_services/critical/sbifida/conditions/spina/diagnosis.html. Accessed on December 12, 2008.

17. "Prenatal Testing Basics: Amniocentesis," by the Editors of *Parents Magazine*, http://www.parents.com/pregnancy/stages/amniocentesis/prenatal-testing-amniocentesis/. Accessed December 13, 2008.

18. New York-Presbyterian Hospital, "Spina Bifida and Spinal Dysraphism," http://www.nyp.org/health/spina-bifida.html. Accessed on December 18, 2008.

19. Kalb, Claudia, "Spotlight on Autism," Newsweek, October 20, 2008, http://www.newsweek.com/id/164790. Accessed on December 19, 2008.

20. Remarks by Governor Sarah Palin on the McCain-Palin Commitment to Children with Special Needs," Arlington, Virginia—McCain-Palin Press Office, Friday, October 24, 2008," *Adventures in Autism*, October 24, 2008,. http://adventuresinautism.blogspot.com/2008/10/sarah-palin-gives-her-first-policy.html. Accessed on December 19, 2008.

21. Goldman, Russell, "Sarah Palin Defends Abortion Stance, Explains 'Bridge to Nowhere' Support" Charles Gibson in exclusive interview, *ABC News Report*, September 12, 2008, http://abcnews.go.com/Politics/Vote2008/story?id=5787748&page=1. Accessed on December 21, 2008.

22. *World Net Daily*, "GOOD NEWS! Mom Rejects Abortion after Down Syndrome Diagnosis Praise for Governor: 'May God give

America more women like her,'" May 20, 2008, 2008, http://www.wnd.com/index.php?fa=PAGE.view&pageId=64876. Accessed on December 22, 2008.

23. "Remarks by Governor Sarah Palin on the McCain-Palin Commitment to Children with Special Needs," Arlington, Virginia—McCain-Palin Press Office, Friday, October 24, 2008, and McCain-Palin Press Office statements delivered via e-mail.

24. Ibid.

25. Goldman, Russell, "Sarah Palin Defends Abortion Stance, Explains 'Bridge to Nowhere' Support" Charles Gibson in exclusive interview, *ABC News Report,* September 12, 2008, http://abcnews.go.com/Politics/Vote2008/story?id=5787748&page=1. Accessed on December 23, 2008.

26. Kane, Paul, "Palin Slashed Funding for Teen Moms," *Washington Post,* September 2, 2008, http://voices.washingtonpost.com/the-trail/2008/09/02/palin_slashed_funding_to_help.html. Accessed on December 23, 2008.

27. Throckmorton, Warren, "Sarah Palin Did Not Slash Funds for Teen Mothers," September 3, 2008, http://wthrockmorton.com/2008/09/03/sarah-palin-did-not-slash-funds-for-teen-mothers/. Accessed on December 24, 2008.

28. Hopkins, Kyle, "Same-Sex Unions, Drugs Get Little Play," *Anchorage Daily News*, August 6, 2006, http://dwb.adn.com/news/politics/elections/governor06/story/8049298p-7942233c.html. Accessed on November 18, 2008.

29. Strange, Hannah, "Who is Sarah Palin?" *Times Online,* August 29, 2008, http://www.timesonline.co.uk/tol/news/world/us_and_americas/article4635147.ece. Accessed on November 19, 2008

30. Brody, David, "Palin Signals Support for Federal Marriage Amendment," Christian News, October 20, 2008, http://www.cbn.com/cbnnews/467179.aspx. Accessed on November 20, 2008.

Chapter 5

PALIN POWER

Sarah Palin emerged on the national political scene using the persona of the country bumpkin with a twist of the wild frontierswoman bearing arms and five children while creating the fresh appeal of a shocking blast of Arctic air.[1] She presented herself in this light for a purpose, and her primary audience was the average American Joe and Joanne who favors God and country. She hired country music singers to introduce her speeches on the campaign trail, and she appeared on the platform hoisting Trig, her infant son, proudly above her head. During the 2008 presidential campaign, Sarah Palin all but kicked up an Alaskan storm.

Palin's down home persona has been compared by journalist Michael Gerson to that of William Jennings Bryan, the Democratic candidate who ran for president in 1896, in 1900, and again in 1908. Bryan made a considerable impact upon America: "[He] never won the presidency in three tries. But his populism transformed the Democratic Party and informed the New Deal, [making] him perhaps the most influential presidential nominee never elected to office."[2] While Bryan ran on the Democratic ticket, Palin was a Republican. But she, as well as John McCain, preferred to be considered a maverick; that is, a candidate not representing the strict party line. This was an attempt to separate herself from the unpopular incumbent president, Republican George W. Bush, whose unending wars in the Middle East and conservative economics had alienated many Americans.

Capturing the energy and excitement of the Republican National Convention where she made her national debut, Palin—like Bryan, as Michael Gerson noted—heralded the "triumph of another backwoods, highly religious populist":

> She praised the honesty and sincerity of small towns; pressed her credentials as a "hockey mom," member of the PTA, and small-town mayor; and railed against the "Washington elite," "power brokers" and (a little close to home) "reporters and commentators." If hats had been in style, they would have been thrown.[3]

Bryan was hailed as The Great Commoner in his day, and in many ways Palin followed suit. Yet along with the common image comes a certain humility and the notion of having little political experience or clout. While Palin was criticized by many as having a lack of experience to run for the vice presidency, Gerson was rare among journalists during the 2008 campaign in conceding that while Palin had served for years as mayor of Wasilla and governor of Alaska, Barack Obama's only political experience was serving in the Illinois state senate and in the U.S. Senate. Gerson suggested that Obama's kind of experience was elitist compared with Palin's, and that in addition to having attained his Ivy League Columbia undergraduate and Harvard law degrees, Obama was a member of "the most exclusive club in America, the Senate."[4] The irony in this is that the Democrats have traditionally been the party of the common people, and the Republicans have represented the interests of wealth in the nation.

If Palin does indeed embody the values of the West as opposed to those of the "coastal elites," she is clearly following in the footsteps not only of Bryan but of Barry Goldwater and Ronald Reagan, appealing to the spirit of American individualism. John Wayne and Randolph Scott would be proud of her, and *The Western Writings of Stephen Crane* would become her manifesto. Clearly, there is something appealing about the courageous spirit of those who venture out west to brave the unknown, and Alaska has indeed been dubbed the last American frontier. If Palin's real appeal is that of the wild woman of the West, author Bob Boze Bell sums up the requirement: "A woman needed guts to live out West. The 'weaker sex' encountered savage, brutal and obnoxious obstacles (and these were just the men!), not to mention mean ol' Mother Nature and a plague or two...the American frontier attracted legions of nonconforming women–mavericks, loners, eccentrics and adventurers. And through it all they kept their sense of humor: 'I've got 350 head of cattle and one son,' said a widowed ranchwoman. 'Don't know which was harder to raise.'"[5] Not every housewife, househusband, or career person today could measure up, but many live vicariously though the adventures of others on the frontier in history, film, and even in politics.

Palin's experience in political office notwithstanding, she was characterized by some as a candidate with little knowledge of the political arena. Some of this enmity came from the Democrats, as mudslinging is par for the course in any election; however, the level of animosity roused among some in the media was truly unprecedented. None of the other candidates were subjected to long interviews with reporters whose agendas appeared to include the intent of discrediting them.

Katie Couric, the former NBC *Today Show* host who had become an evening anchor for *CBS Evening News* on September 5, 2006, conducted an interview with Sarah Palin on September 24, 2008. Couric's questions were very specific, and Palin did not have some of the answers at her fingertips, which made her appear to be less than knowledgeable:

Couric: You've said, quote, "John McCain will reform the way Wall Street does business." Other than supporting stricter regulations of Fannie Mae and Freddie Mac two years ago, can you give us any more example of his leading the charge for more oversight?

Palin: I think that the example that you just cited, with his warnings two years ago about Fannie and Freddie— that, that's paramount. That's more than a heck of a lot of other senators and representatives did for us.[6]

In another exchange, Couric repeatedly pressed Palin to describe examples that demonstrated McCain's commitment to reforming the financial

industry. Emphasizing his reputation as a "maverick," Palin noted Mc-
Cain's general willingness to withstand resistance from both political parties as he has called for government reforms. Unsatisfied with her answer,
Couric repeated the question, adding that Palin had accused Obama of
empty rhetoric without gaining results. The following exchange ensued:

> Palin: I can give you examples of things that John McCain
>   has done, that has shown his foresight, his pragmatism,
>   and his leadership abilities. And that is what America
>   needs today.
>
> Couric: I'm just going to ask you one more time—not to be-
>   labor the point. Specific examples in his 26 years of
>   pushing for more regulation.
>
> Palin: I'll try to find you some and I'll bring them to you.[7]

Katie Couric may have had a hidden agenda in her approach to questioning Palin. Apparently, her ratings had been dropping considerably
since she took over the Evening News position. According to the *Wall
Street Journal,*

> After two years of record-low ratings, both CBS News executives
> and people close to Katie Couric say that the "CBS Evening News"
> anchor is likely to leave the network well before her contract ex-
> pires in 2011—possibly soon after the presidential inauguration
> early next year. Ms. Couric isn't even halfway through her five-
> year contract with CBS, which began in June 2006 and pays an
> annual salary of around $15 million....Excluding several weeks of
> her tenure, Ms. Couric never bested the ratings of interim anchor
> Bob Schieffer, who was named to host the broadcast temporarily
> after "Evening News" anchor Dan Rather left the newscast.[8]

In a second interview with both Palin and McCain which was broadcast on September 30, 2008, Couric was accused by both candidates
of employing "gotcha journalism" techniques in the first interview.
McCain seemed to be scolding Couric, and she appeared embarrassed
when he spoke to her:

> Couric: Over the weekend, Gov. Palin, you said the U.S. should
>   absolutely launch cross-border attacks from Afghanistan

into Pakistan to, quote, "stop the terrorists from coming any further in." Now, that's almost the exact position that Barack Obama has taken and that you, Sen. McCain, have criticized as something you do not say out loud. So, Gov. Palin, are you two on the same page on this?

Palin: We had a great discussion with President Zardari as we talked about what it is that America can and should be doing together to make sure that the terrorists do not cross borders and do not ultimately put themselves in a position of attacking America again or her allies. And we will do what we have to do to secure the United States of America and her allies.

Couric: Is that something you shouldn't say out loud, Sen. McCain?

John McCain: Of course not. But, look, I understand this day and age of "gotcha" journalism.... In a conversation with someone who you didn't hear... the question very well, you don't know the context of the conversation, grab a phrase. Gov. Palin and I agree that you don't announce that you're going to attack another country...

Couric: Are you sorry you said it?

McCain: ...and the fact...

Couric: Governor?

McCain: Wait a minute. Before you say, "Is she sorry she said it," this was a "gotcha" sound bite that, look...

Couric: It wasn't a "gotcha." She was talking to a voter.

McCain: No, she was in a conversation with a group of people and talking back and forth. And I can tell you that I would say, if I was asked, of course we have to do what's necessary to protect America. The question is, is whether you make an outright public announcement the way that Sen. Obama did. And I don't think you do that. And... I'll let Gov. Palin speak for herself.

Palin: In fact, you're absolutely right on. In the context, this was … a voter, a constituent, hollering out a question from across an area asking, "What are you gonna do about Pakistan? You better have an answer to Pakistan." I said we're gonna do what we have to do to protect the United States of America.

Couric: But you were pretty specific about what you wanted to do, cross-border …

Palin: Well, as Sen. McCain is suggesting here, also, never would our administration get out there and show our cards to terrorists, in this case, to enemies and let them know what the game plan was, not when that could ultimately adversely affect a plan to keep America secure.

Couric: What did you learn from that experience?

Palin: That this is all about "gotcha" journalism. A lot of it is. (laughter) But that's okay, too.

McCain: We don't mind. We just …

Palin: That's okay.

McCain: That's life.[9]

Katie Couric required specific answers from Palin in the September 24 interview, yet when she gave specifics in answering a question from a persistent person in an audience, Couric criticized her for it. Both McCain and Palin perceived an attempt to entrap Palin in either case. There seemed to have been some competition on the part of Couric with Palin during the interviews that she conducted. Palin was making the news while Couric was reporting it.

In the case of Sarah Palin, the press was exceedingly irritated by the fact that she was unavailable for interviews at the beginning of the campaign, although the Republicans had used this "cocoon strategy" before when President Bush was the incumbent. Yet there were no such ramifications for him: "Bush's current incumbent strategy is also a 'cocoon' strategy. It insulates the candidate from a press eager for, and versed in, the methods of 'gotcha' journalism. When you are ahead, don't give your candidate opportunities to stumble."[10]

Todd Palin holds the Bible as his wife Sarah is sworn in as governor of Alaska, in Fairbanks, on December 4, 2006. AP Photo/Al Grillo.

Palin's one characteristic that was both her blessing and her curse during the 2008 campaign is her phenomenal beauty. It attracted people to her yet simultaneously caused a huge commotion while she was running for national office. The stereotype of a beautiful but stupid woman became the chorus of her detractors in the media who focused on one or two snafus in the Couric interviews yet paid little attention to all of the questions that she answered with clarity, knowledge, and the expertise she had gained in public office, especially as presented in Palin's September 2008 interviews with Charlie Gibson on the ABC network. The press also played down her successful vice presidential debate with Joe Biden. However, even after the end of the election, some were repeating the claim of an anonymous source that Palin didn't know that Africa was a continent. Several of her supporters who have spent time with her have vehemently refuted this accusation. Greta Van Susteren of Fox News came to her defense on this issue:

> The sniping at Gov. Palin after the election by 'anonymous' sources is rotten.... I have said over and over and over again, it is

our job in journalism to be aggressive in challenging politicians...
but it is not right to gratuitously trash someone...and worse, it
becomes 'conventional wisdom' giving some journalists blinders—
meaning they don't step back and investigate for themselves but
rather go with the so called conventional wisdom...that is not
fair to the politician and is not a good for journalism or the First
Amendment."[11]

In an interview with Van Susteren, Jane Swift, former governor of
Massachusetts, spoke highly of Palin's intelligence and ability to respond quickly to questions. Swift discussed the double standard in
dealing with the way that candidates present themselves. She stated
that women candidates are treated differently than men in the areas
of appearance and personality. This kind of scrutiny disregards the fact
that "this dynamic woman" is the governor of, as Greta Van Susteren
chimed in, "the largest state in the country," a mother, and an inspiration to young women.[12] Elaine Lafferty—a former editor-in-chief of
Ms. Magazine as well as a feminist activist who spent time traveling
with Sarah Palin on the campaign trail contributing to her speech on
women's rights—noted that she is "very smart," well informed about
the war in Afghanistan and the Taliban, and has been managing Alaska's $4 billion in exports, dealing with both China and Japan. Lafferty
spoke about the notion that Palin spent hours in department stores
shopping for clothes, pointing out that anyone who had seen her daily
schedule would know that this was impossible.[13] Palin's campaign appearances, announced to the press by the McCain/Palin Campaign in
Arlington, Virginia, confirm that she often spoke in more than one
location daily. Lafferty commented that Palin traveled between these
locations in a plane that was very crowded and uncomfortable.[14]

Great beauty inspires great envy, and Palin became the butt of jokes
among many in the media but also average citizens working in offices
around the country as well as some of her own security personnel on the
campaign trail. A portrayal by television personality Tina Fey (who has
a remarkable resemblance to Palin and captured her accent and inflec-
tion) on Saturday Night Live in a series beginning on September, 15,
2008, was witty and poignant yet exaggerated her faults. Others were
less skilled. Palin waded through the tide of these onslaughts, be they

At a National Governors Association meeting in Acme, Michigan, in July 2007, Governor Sarah Palin measures siding for a demonstration Habitat for Humanity home. Michigan Governor Jennifer Granholm and her son Jack are in the background at right. AP Photo/John L. Russell.

humorous or mean spirited. Many attacks were in fact vicious, and others were sexist in nature. On the Internet and in the tabloids, her head appeared on a stranger's body in a scanty swimsuit, and her clothing on the campaign trail became an arena for exaggerated attacks (and not just among Democrats) even after the Democrats had won the election. Male celebrity Matt Damon raved against Palin in Internet videos. Anger and hostility filled the air because a woman from the far Northwest was attempting to gain access to the White House, a house where women have only been welcome as sidekicks, party planners, and stand-by-your-man women. Palin was turned into a living cartoon in a way that no vice presidential candidate had ever been before.

Underneath the pioneer persona, the beauty queen image, and the sex object was a woman of striking intelligence and strength of spirit. Yet Palin was championed only by a handful of feminists, while the National Organization of Women chose to support the Democratic ticket with two men running for office.

Elaine Lafferty's article "Sarah Palin Is a Brainiac" illustrates that she is much more intelligent than she was given credit for by many on national television. After advising the McCain/Palin campaign on issues pertaining to women's rights, Lafferty stated that Palin demonstrated her ability to '[ask] questions and [probe] linkages and logic' and takes the rare stance of 'a woman who knows exactly who she is,' remarking about her "photographic memory" and attesting to having seen it in action. Lafferty believes that Palin supports women's rights, deeply and passionately: "Yes, Palin is a harder sell, she looks and sounds different, and one can rightfully oppose her based on abortion policies. If you only vote on how a person personally feels about abortion, you will never want her to darken your door. If you care about anything else, she will continue to intrigue you.... Will Palin's time come next week? I don't know. But her time will come."[15]

Others came to Palin's defense and saw beyond the bimbo blitz to which she was being subjected, asserting that questions concerning whether it would be possible for her to manage a large family while holding national office were sexist. Reporter Robin Abcarian recorded the reaction of prominent members of the McCain-Palin team: in response to speculation that Palin might have trouble juggling the vice presidency and her family obligations, McCain aide Steve Schmidt stated, "'Frankly ... I can't imagine that question being asked of a man. I think it's offensive, and I think a lot of women will find it offensive,'" and Abcarian quoted Cindy McCain, the prospective first lady, as telling Katie Couric in an interview that "[Sarah Palin] will be a marvelous vice president, and she is already a marvelous mother.... I think most of the people asking the questions wouldn't be asking this if it were a man."[16] At the Republican National Convention, former New York mayor Rudolph W. Giuliani, who was the keynote speaker, "reacted with outrage to the question of Palin's balancing act," querying, "When do they ever ask a man that question?"[17]

And Phyllis Schlafly, "the 84-year-old archetypal anti-feminist, thinks people fretting about whether Palin can do it all should just pipe down. 'People who don't have children, or who only have one or two, don't comprehend what it's like to have five,' said Schlafly, who was on the convention floor this week. 'I had six children.... I ran for Congress. An organized mother puts it all together.'"[18]

*Republican vice presidential nominee Sarah Palin greets
enthusiastic young supporters at an October 23, 2008,
campaign stop in Troy, Ohio. AP Photo/Skip Peterson.*

Sarah Palin addressed these questions herself in an interview with
television news anchor Charlie Gibson. When Gibson asked her
whether voters might doubt her ability to fulfill the duties of the vice
presidency as well as those to her family, Palin responded:

> I don't know. I'm lucky to have been brought up in a family where
> gender has never been an issue. I'm a product of Title 9, also,
> where we had equality in schools that was just being ushered in
> with sports and with equal opportunity for education, all of my
> life.... I'm part of that generation, where that question is kind of
> irrelevant, because it's accepted. Of course you can be the vice
> president and you can raise a family.... I'm the governor and I'm
> raising a family. I've been a mayor and have raised a family. I've
> owned a business and we've raised a family.... What people have

asked me when I was—when I learned I was pregnant, "Gosh, how are you going to be the governor and have a baby in office, too," and I replied back then, as I would today, "'I'll do it the same way the other governors have done it when they've either had a baby in office or raised a family.' Granted, they're men, but do it the same way that they do it."[19]

Palin went on to empathize with the "struggle" and "internal questions" that working mothers regularly encounter; she regards the decision to be a stay-at-home mom, a part-time worker, or a full-time employee as a personal choice.

Sarah Palin may be viewed as a role model for women with children returning to work, and even though she takes a conservative stand on many of the issues, she nevertheless represents the movement of women taking an active role in the highest offices of the American government. Indeed, "when historians write about the 2008 election, it may be remembered as the year of the woman."[20] According to Dee Dee Myers, former press secretary to Bill Clinton, in an interview with Daniel Scarpinato of the *Arizona Star,* "Gov. Palin's candidacy has created an interesting discussion about identity politics. Here you have a conservative woman who in many ways is living a progressive lifestyle—not having to choose between work and family.... Even though I disagree with Palin's politics, I think she's good for women."[21]

Sarah Palin succeeded in two previous campaigns: for mayor of Wasilla in 1996 and for governor of Alaska in 2006. And while the Republicans did not win the 2008 election, Sarah Palin made it clear in her postelection appearances that she will remain on the political scene in the future. Dee Dee Myers captures it succinctly: "I think one of the things that's really important is role models for women. Nothing succeeds like success."[22] Palin has succeeded in the past, which is a realistic indication of her future successes.

NOTES

1. *Newsweek,* "PALIN•TOL•OGY," September 7, 2008 11:52 A.M., http://blog.newsweek.com/blogs/pr/archive/2008/09/07/newsweek-cover-release-palin-tol-ogy.aspx. "Palin's personal story taps one of the

great American myths—the hardy woman of the frontier, God-fearing and determined to succeed against the odds." Accessed on October 6, 2008.

2. Gerson, Michael, "Starbucks Does Not Equal Savvy: What We Talk about When We Talk about Experience," *Newsweek,* September 29, 2008. Vol. 152, Iss. 13, http://www.newsweek.com/id/160085. Accessed on October 8, 2008.

3. Ibid.

4. Ibid.

5. Bell, Bob Boze, "Wild Women of the West," *History Net* (originally appeared in the April 1997 issue of *Wild West* magazine, http://www.historynet.com/wild-women-of-the-west.htm). Accessed on October 9, 2008.

6. *CBS Evening News,* Anchor Katie Couric Interviews Alaska's Governor on the Ailing Economy, "One-On-One With Sarah Palin," New York, September 24, 2008, http://www.cbsnews.com/stories/2008/09/24/eveningnews/main4476173.shtml. Accessed on October 10, 2008.

7. Ibid.

8. Dana, Rebecca, "CBS News, Katie Couric Are Likely to Part Ways," *Wall Street Journal,* April 10, 2008, http://online.wsj.com/article/SB120778369100203247.html?mod=hpp_us_whats_news. Accessed on October 11, 2008.

9. *CBS News,* "Transcript: Palin And McCain Interview: More In-Depth Answers to Questions Katie Couric Asked McCain and Palin on the Broadcast," p. 2, September 30, 2008, http://www.cbsnews.com/stories/2008/09/30/eveningnews/main4490788_page2.shtml. Accessed on October 12, 2008.

10. Spencer, Stuart K., "Bush Behaves Like an Incumbent," *Los Angeles Times,* March 27, 1988. Accessed on October 12, 2008.

11. Fox News, *On the Record,* "The Trashing of Governor Palin," Greta Van Susteren, November 7, 2008, http://gretawire.foxnews.com/2008/11/07/the-trashing-of-gov-palin/. Accessed on November 15, 2008.

12. Ibid.

13. Lafferty, Elaine, "Sarah Palin's a Brainiac," *Daily Beast,* October 27, 2008, www.thedailybeast.com/blogs-and-stories/2008–10–27/sarah-palins-a-brainiac/1/—94k. Accessed on October 28, 2008.

14. Ibid.

15. Lafferty, Elaine, "Sarah Palin's a Brainiac," *Daily Beast*, October 27, 2008, www.thedailybeast.com/blogs-and-stories/2008–10–27/sarah-palins-a-brainiac/1/—94k. Accessed on October 29, 2008.

16. Abcarian, Robin, "Insiders See 'New Feminism,'" *Los Angeles Times*, September 4, 2008, http://articles.latimes.com/2008/sep/04/nation/na-motherhood4. Accessed on October 28, 2008.

17. Ibid.

18. Ibid.

19. *ABC News*, "Excerpts: Charlie Gibson Interviews GOP Vice Presidential Candidate Sarah Palin," September 13, 2008, http://abcnews.go.com/Politics/Vote2008/Story?id=5789483&page=2. Accessed on October 20, 2008.

20. Scarpinato, Daniel, "Ex-Clinton Aide on Politics and Sexism," *Arizona Daily Star,* Tucson, distributed by McClatchy-Tribune Information Services, September 25, 2008, ABI/INFORM Dateline database. (Document ID: 1561018361). Accessed on October 20, 2008.

21. Ibid.

22. Ibid.

Chapter 6

POLITICAL RÉSUMÉ

Sarah Palin's impressive political ascent heralded her August 2008 selection as Republican candidate for vice president. While her sudden emergence on the national political scene appeared almost miraculous to many, she had had her political gaze focused on Washington for some time. As mayor of Wasilla, she even hired a law firm to lobby for Wasilla's interests in Washington. She maintained contact with John Bitney, a former high school friend and government employee whom she had fired from his post when she took office as governor and who later became chief of staff to the speaker of the Alaska House. Bitney was aware that Palin had considered the possibility of working her way into office in Washington. Remarkably, however, it was a little-known blogger, Adam Brickley, who initiated an online campaign to support Palin as a vice presidential candidate.

After taking office as governor, Palin had begun to develop new relationships with an influential group of conservative Washington insiders. Told that they would arrive in Juneau in summer 2007 on two cruise-ship excursions, one sponsored by the *Weekly Standard* and the other by the *National Review*—both conservative political journals—she invited both groups to dine at the governor's mansion.[1] At a dinner and later at a luncheon she hosted, she fed them Alaskan fish and charmed them with her intelligence and confidence. She made a particularly strong impression on commentator William Kristol, who wrote for the *Weekly Standard* and at the time was also an Op-Ed columnist for the *New York Times*. Kristol was highly impressed by Palin's charisma and vigorously supported her in Washington. He also played a large role in her selection as vice presidential candidate. Kristol was not the only one infatuated by Palin: *Washington Post* columnist Michael Gerson referred to her as a cross between Annie Oakley and Joan of Arc,[2] suggesting that her public appeal would be on a grand scale. Indeed, it was neither miraculous nor accidental that she was chosen to run alongside McCain.

While her physical appearance influenced some—to the extent that she was referred to as a "beauty queen" rather than a potential candidate—it was Palin's track record in office that spurred the leaders of the Republican Party to convince John McCain to accept her as a running mate. McCain preferred Senator Joe Lieberman of Connecticut as his running mate; however, key Republican Party advisers convinced him that he would have the best chance of winning the election with Palin at his side. In general, her record as a reformer, movement conservative, and principled leader, and her ability to reach independent voters, convinced party leaders that she would be the best choice in the long run. Specific policies and actions in office played a large role in persuading detractors that she would be the best candidate, including selling the governor's jet acquired by her predecessor in office, abandoning the much-criticized $223 million "Bridge to Nowhere" project, formulating and putting in effect new ethics standards, opposing wasteful fiscal spending, and supporting fiscal responsibility. Additionally, Palin had championed tax cuts, defended human life under the Second Amendment, and supported drilling in the Arctic National Wildlife Refuge as well as expanding domestic oil supplies throughout the country to create a more independent America.

Sarah Palin's finest hour was perhaps during the 2008 Republican National Convention when she accepted the nomination for the vice presidency. It was before she was attacked for what some considered her lack of intelligence and experience and before her wardrobe became a major issue of the campaign. At the convention, she wore a simple gray dress with a short strand of pearls, looking far more like a corporate executive at a dinner meeting than a nominee for the second-highest elective office in the United States—a decision that appeared to be intentional. She looked professional yet down home and as ordinary as a business woman at the PTA.

Her speech, however, was as hard-hitting as any of her future campaign speeches, and she began by praising the leadership that John McCain could provide. Voters, she said, would favor him because of his 22 years of military service. She then proceeded to praise and honor her eldest son, Track, who was about to deploy to Iraq, and she also mentioned her nephew Kasey, who was already serving in the Gulf. She introduced her other children by name, along with her husband, and focused immediately upon her special-needs newborn, Trig, a Down syndrome baby. Her convention speech was the first time Palin used the axiom, "Special-needs children inspire a special love," which would become a staple of her speeches on the campaign trail. She promised parents of special-needs children that they would have a friend in the White House if she were elected. Palin also praised her husband as a member of the Steel Workers' Union and noted that they had met in high school. She was proud of her working-class background and introduced her parents, Sally and Chuck Heath, as having both worked in the local elementary school. She indicated that it was from her parents that she had gained her confidence that in America, "every woman can walk through every door of opportunity."

After recounting her rise up the political ladder from hockey mom to mayor and then governor, Palin took a pointed shot at Democratic presidential candidate Barack Obama: "I guess a small-town mayor is sort of like a 'community organizer,' except that you have actual responsibilities." She added that small-town folk don't understand a candidate who praises working people in their presence but complains at other times that they "cling to guns or religion," lifting a phrase from a speech made by Obama at a San Francisco fundraiser during his campaign for the Democratic nomination. Palin remarked that John McCain was always the same man wherever he went. She stated that she planned to go to Washington not to associate with the political establishment but to serve her country. Her definition of the right reasons included challenging the status quo, serving the common good, and leaving the nation a better place than she found it.

Palin then began to tout her accomplishments in Alaska, including taking on the "good ol' boys network" in Juneau—which, in fact, she had done in several of her previous political posts, notably as governor by slashing the budget for the governor's personal perquisites, having not only sold the luxury jet but also firing her driver and chef. Consequently, she could assert that the state budget was now under control. Palin also mentioned that she told Congress that if her state wanted a "Bridge to Nowhere," the funds would come from the state rather than the national coffers.

Palin then focused on issues concerning national security by showing how she planned to further develop U.S. natural oil and gas resources to avoid the necessity of relying on foreign oil, especially from the Middle East. Once again, she held Obama accountable for avoiding the word *victory* when speaking of the war in Iraq and for planning to raise taxes, especially for small-business owners. She compared Obama's and McCain's idealism: Obama as a high-flown speechmaker and McCain as an activist who would bring about change. She pointed out that McCain was the only candidate who had in actuality fought for his country as opposed to Obama's promise to do so.

Palin concluded her speech by referring to John McCain's bravery as a POW during the Vietnam War. She conveyed the anecdote about McCain's positivism and strength, as viewed by Tom Moe of Lancaster, Ohio, a fellow prisoner-of-war who would look through a pinhole in his cell door at John McCain as he was brought back each day to his four-by-six-foot cell after interrogations. Tom saw McCain smiling and holding his thumbs up, indicating that they were going to make it through their horrible ordeal. Palin stated, "For a season, a gifted speaker can inspire with his words. But for a lifetime, John McCain has inspired with his deeds."

As the campaign progressed, unfortunately, the love-hate relationship Americans have with female beauty played a role. While Rush Limbaugh praised her as a "babe," during the campaign, it was her gender and beauty that was most frequently attacked, including everything from her role as mother of five children to her wardrobe. After his choice of Palin as his running mate, John McCain had to face a reality of American politics: women are considered unqualified no matter their qualifications. The intense focus on Palin's appearance, her manner of speaking, and the minor details she could or could not recall or chose not to divulge on the spur of the moment ensured Palin's political skills and accomplishments were relatively underappreciated.

Palin billed herself as "just your average hockey mom who signed up for the PTA because I wanted to make my kids' public education better. When I ran for city council, I didn't need focus groups and voter profiles because I knew those voters and knew their families too."[3] However, she is a smart, innovative, and savvy politician with goals far beyond the Alaskan tundra. While the 2012 election remained in the distant future, a December 2008 CNN/Opinion Research poll of Republicans nationwide placed Palin in the lead as the GOP's choice for a presidential candidate: "The 2008 GOP vice presidential nominee, got a 67% "very/somewhat likely" score."[4]

According to journalist Nathan Thornburgh, "Palin has proved to be a shrewd political operator who slyly fought her way upstream through her state's cutthroat politics, someone more formidable than her image might suggest—and more than some in her own party are willing to

Sarah Palin beams at her audience from the podium during an October 26, 2008, campaign speech at the Asheville, North Carolina, Civic Center. Shutterstock/Maria Nebritov.

acknowledge. For all her savvy, or maybe because of it, she has been launched headlong into the role of a lifetime, for which almost nothing could have prepared her."[5] Yet Palin's background in local Alaskan politics did prepare her to initiate an exemplary vice presidential campaign, one in which despite the slings and arrows of outrageous criticism, she bounced back directly after the Democratic victory and appeared on national television with the same down-home chutzpah that she had brought to the campaign trail.

Palin's first foray into the political arena was in 1992, when she was 28 years old. She ran for public office in the Wasilla City Council on the suggestion of City Councilman Nick Carney. She had become familiar with several local town politicians, including Mayor John Stein and police chief Irl Stambaugh, at a step aerobics class.[6] For the Palins, campaigning was a family affair: she and Todd pulled their two children, Track, who was four at the time, and Bristol, who was two, in a red wagon and went door to door.[7] Although she had lived in Wasilla most of her life, she promoted herself as a "New face, new voice" for "a progressive Wasilla." She won the election by 530 to 310 against John Hartrick.

Once in office, Palin immediately recognized that she had joined what she called a "good old boys network" but was destined to bring about change. Mayor Stein and Nick Carney had told her: "You'll learn quick; just listen to us."[8] Palin's response was to vote against a pay raise for the mayor and against Nick Carney's ordinance requiring Wasilla residents to use his garbage pickup service. She felt that residents should have the choice to use the town dump if they so desired.[9]

Palin ran for a second term and defeated R'Nita Rogers, yet she still felt that she was up against political cronyism that was not in the best interests of her constituents. Mayor Stein had been in office since 1987, and he ran for a fourth term in 1996. Palin took a step forward, challenged city hall, and won. She once again presented herself as a breath of fresh air which would replace "stale leadership" and offered to save the taxpayers money by taking a pay cut herself. She was not afraid of publicly criticizing an administration that had been in place for many years, and she was capable of handling the censure she received, including remarks concerning her young age of 32 as well as her lack of experience for the job. This theme of her youth and inexperience would follow her all the way to the 2008 vice presidential campaign and beyond. Yet as she climbed each rung of the political ladder, she surpassed expectations, and by 2008 it was reported that her approval rating had risen above 80 percent, the highest popularity rating among governors in the United States.[10]

Palin posed for a photo shoot for an advertisement with local Republican legislators, and her detractors claimed that this created divisive party politics in a nonpartisan race. Palin chose to conduct her campaign on issues she believed would be of importance to Alaskans. She introduced unconventional topics such as abortion and gun control into a mayoral race that had traditionally been conducted like a friendly town meeting. Mayor Stein appeared to be displeased with Palin's outside endorsements and the unprecedented issues which she had brought to the political scene in Wasilla.

Nathan Thornburgh describes the conflicts that developed during the 1996 campaign: "Palin often describes that 1996 race as having been a fight against the old boys' club. Stein's memory is different. 'It got to the extent that—I don't remember who it was now—but some national antiabortion outfit sent little pink cards to voters in Wasilla endorsing her,' he says. Chas St. George, a Palin friend who worked on Stein's campaign, says he has no reason to dispute Stein's recollection of events but doesn't remember Palin's conduct as beyond the pale. 'Our tax coffers were starting to grow,' he says. 'John was for expanding services, and Sarah wasn't. That's what the race was about.'"[11]

During her first two weeks in office, Nick Carney overtly offered to make her job difficult, and the police chief, Irl Stambaugh, was unhappy with her appointment. Heads began to roll as Palin replaced former officials in the city government. She asked for the resignations of several people in office: the director of public works, Jack Felton; the director of finance, Duane Dvorak; and Mary Ellen Emmons, the librarian. She eliminated the position of the city museum's director, from which John Cooper had resigned. According to former Mayor Stein, Palin wanted to ban certain books from the local library, apparently because "some voters thought they had inappropriate language in them."[12]

Palin was aware of the power of the press long before her vice presidential campaign. In an attempt to protect her career and her goals, she required department heads to seek approval from her office before talking with reporters. This was regarded as a "gag order" by the local paper, the *Frontiersman*.[13] While many of the people she had fired had been loyal to Stein, Palin chose to surround herself with those whom she believed would further her plans for the city of Wasilla, and even though she was criticized for it, she filled the position of deputy administrator, hiring John Cramer for the job which had been vacant for the previous 18 months. Several months later, she fired police chief Irl Stambaugh, who "alleg[ed] that Palin fired him in part at the behest of the National Rifle Association because he had opposed a concealed-gun law that the NRA supported."[14] Palin has maintained a strong relationship with the National Rifle Association throughout her political career. Stambaugh eventually filed a lawsuit for "contract violation, wrongful termination, and gender discrimination," which he lost some time later.

Once she had moved into office and the dust of her reorganization had settled, Palin fulfilled her campaign promises. She took a $3,800 pay cut, reducing her salary from $68,000 to $64,200. She reduced property taxes by $800,000 and eliminated personal property taxes and a business inventory tax. Voters passed her $5.5 million road and sewer bond which brought new commercial development to the area. Floating a bond is often the best way to make material improvements in any organization or governing body. Some taxpayers complained about the bond, yet the majority of voters were pleased with the results. The town of Wasilla was growing: "People living in Anchorage began to see it as a desirable place to live. Before long, 'big box' retailers wanted to locate there as well. With retail options improving, people in town no longer had to drive to Anchorage in the dead of winter to buy groceries; they could shop right down the street from their house and be back in less than half the time."[15]

In the 1999 mayoral election, Palin once again defeated John Stein, who ran against her and criticized the $5.5 million bond. Palin believed it was essential for the growth of Wasilla, and it had proved to be an excellent move.

While Palin served as mayor, two other prospects arose for her. In 2002, while still mayor, she ran for lieutenant governor and also attempted to gain a seat in the U.S. Senate. She lost the lieutenant governor race, apparently because she had not spent enough money on the campaign. Upon his inauguration as governor of Alaska in December 2002, Frank Murkowski appointed his own daughter, Lisa, as his successor to his Senate seat, which he had held for 22 years. Palin later turned down two job offers: a position in the governor's office as commissioner of the Department of Commerce and the job of state parks director. When Murkowski offered her a spot with the Alaska Oil and Gas Conservation Commission (AOGCC) in 2003, however, she accepted. Palin believed that this would put her at the heart of the most vital agency in Alaska as the state's budget is highly dependent upon oil.

The political climate in Wasilla was undergoing a change: "By 2002 the area around Wasilla had begun to shift from Democrat to Republican as more conservative voters moved out of Anchorage and into the Mat-Su Valley. A number of new Republican candidates had won election to the Alaska legislature. As Sarah approached the end of her second term as mayor, she was an obvious candidate for statewide office. What had begun as a mother's desire to contribute to a better place in which to rear her children had grown a little larger."[16] Palin gave birth to her daughter Piper Indy during her last year as mayor of Wasilla. By this time she was juggling four children and an ever-growing political career. She was able to do this because not only her parents but also her two sisters were helping her. Palin's experience working as Alaska Oil and Gas Conservation commissioner would be invaluable when she ran for the vice presidency years later.

Palin's knowledge and position on environmental issues regarding offshore drilling would be criticized by some, yet she was well informed of the value of developing American oil and gas resources as a means of protecting against further terrorist actions against the United States. During her 2008 campaign speeches, she used the slogan "Drill, Baby, Drill" to show her support for further development of Alaska's natural resources. Nevertheless, environmentalists and some Democratic activists criticized her for her association with big oil companies. They oppose her support for drilling in areas which might adversely affect the environment, and they dislike her skepticism of alternative energy sources. Palin has also been attacked for her opposition to listing polar bears as an endangered species. In actuality, if the bears were listed, then drilling and running the pipeline in certain areas would become impossible. Daniel J. Weiss, senior fellow at the

Center for American Progress, remarked that "Palin may be new, but her big oil energy agenda is very old-fashioned."[17]

Washington Post columnist Steve Mufson spoke with Palin in May 2008 about her views on big oil, offshore drilling, and a proposed new $30 billion natural gas pipeline, a delayed project that Palin had championed. Palin presented her support for the natural gas pipeline as demonstrating her independence from big oil. In actuality, more than 80 percent of Alaska's state budget is garnered from oil and gas tax and royalty revenues. Citizens of Alaska receive a check from the state for the dividends reaped from their share of these revenues.

There has been some conflict, however, regarding oil versus gas in Alaska. Up until recently, oil has been king in the 49th state. Gas would provide a level of competition for the major oil conglomerates that dominate the industry in the region. Palin has lobbied for the $30 billion Trans-Alaska natural gas pipeline even though her husband, Todd, works for one of the largest oil firms in the area, BP. The natural gas pipeline project would not only benefit the major corporations but would also include smaller companies as well, introducing a new level of competition in the area.

In her May 2008 interview with Mufson, Palin stated, "Getting this huge supply flowing is key for our national security and energy independence.... There are other companies besides our oil producers who want the opportunity and vehicle to get gas to market."[18] Palin put her state's money where her mouth was. She managed to get $500 million from the state of Alaska to start the project, contingent upon Trans-Canada's commitment to producing the same amount of initial funding. The ongoing project may take more than 10 years to finish; the big oil companies in the area which also control the natural gas supplies have continued to insist that the pipeline is not financially feasible.

Palin's main interest regarding the project is not to protect the profits of a handful of oil firms. Rather, she has said, she is concerned with protecting the bottom line of the state of Alaska: "I'm not anti-industry, I'm not anti-production. The oil company chief executives I respect are doing what the shareholders have mandated that CEO to do: look out for their bottom line. My bottom line for the state is to do the same for Alaska's shareholders. The people of Alaska own the resources. I have to look after their interests."[19] This, she maintains, illustrates her independence from the concerns of big business.

TransCanada was awarded the license for the project. However, BP has expressed concern about the quality of work that would be performed by TransCanada in Alaska: "It is clearly in our interest as gas lease holders and prospective shippers to make sure this line is done right and managed efficiently." Ironically, BP was responsible for a massive oil spill on the North Slope in March 2006. Over 200,000 gallons of oil poured out of BP pipelines. The cause of the spill was later found to be corrosion resulting from lack of routine maintenance.[20]

BP and ConocoPhillips formed Denali, their own company, to build a natural gas pipeline, posing serious competition for the TransCanada project. While TransCanada has laid tens of thousands of miles of pipeline elsewhere, there are concerns about its ability to meet the Alaskan challenge. Moreover, there is some question about whether Alaskan citizens will benefit from the proceeds. Now that the state has put up half a billion dollars for the project, some wonder whether it will ever be completed; however, supporters are optimistic. Tony Palmer, Trans-Canada's vice president, has stated, "None of those parties [BP, Cono-coPhillips, and Exxon Mobil] have committed their gas to any pipeline at the moment.... We will be doing all we can to attract potential customers."[21] Supporters of Palin laud her efforts to limit the influence of the big oil companies' corner on the market.

According to journalist Kent Garber, even Democratic presidential candidate Barack Obama, before Palin's nomination, supported the natural gas pipeline project as having the potential for "delivering clean natural gas and creating good jobs in the process."[22] Apparently, Palin's experience as a mother has taught her that you don't reward bad behavior. By producing our own resources and becoming less dependent upon foreign oil sources, the United States would kill two birds with one stone. We would provide more of our own energy and simultaneously deprive more or less hostile oil-producing countries of revenue from our purchase of oil. According to Palin, the United States should not conduct business with our enemies, thus placing a kind of embargo on foreign oil.[23]

Palin's attempts to limit the excessive power of oil companies in Alaska goes back to her time with the Alaska Oil and Gas Conservation Commission, the purpose of which is to regulate the state's energy industries. While Randy Ruedrich, then Alaska Republican Party chairman, was a member of the commission, there were some concerns about a conflict of interest on his part regarding his partisan activities on behalf of Republican candidates for elective office as well as additional concerns about the fact that he was also receiving deferred compensation from two companies by which he had previously been employed, BP and Doyon Drilling.[24] Both firms were under investigation for North Slope environmental violations. Another controversy in which Ruedrich was involved concerned land leases under the homes of citizens in the community of Sutton. The land lease situation was serious, especially for home owners who had not been informed that coal-bed methane development would take place on the state-owned land located directly below their homes. Citizens were concerned about contamination of the water as well as the drilling.[25] Even though he was a member of the commission having oversight of the project, Ruedrich contacted Republicans asking for their support of the project. Extracting natural gas from the Alaskan terrain is supported by Palin and her constituents, but extracting it in residential areas is another matter.

Eventually, the *Anchorage Daily News* reported that Ruedrich had also worked with a law firm that supported the development of coal-bed methane development. Shortly thereafter, Ruedrich resigned. Upon the request of Assistant Attorney General Paul Lyle, Palin continued to search for incriminating evidence against Ruedrich; however, she was instructed to keep quiet about her findings and to avoid the media's requests for further information. Palin had reported Ruedrich's behavior by filing more than a dozen complaints up the chain of command. She also spoke to Ruedrich directly about it, but the situation remained the same.[26] The good-old-boys' network in Wasilla had been difficult; however, the network she encountered here was far more daunting.

Palin herself resigned from the commission shortly thereafter in an attempt to protect her own reputation. Ruedrich later admitted to ethics violations and was fined $12,000 for a variety of infractions including "engaging in partisan activity, improperly disclosing a confidential legal document to a lobbyist, and conducting partisan political business from his state office."[27]

As popular dissatisfaction with Murkowski's administration grew, both Palin and a Democratic legislator, Eric Croft, complained to the personnel board about the state attorney general, Gregg Renkes.[28] It was at this point that Palin herself wrote to the *Anchorage Daily News*: "It's said the only difference between a hockey mom and a pit bull is lipstick. So with lipstick on, the gloves come off in answering administration accusations."[29]

Palin criticized Murkowski for using state funds to hire an attorney to investigate his friend and campaign manager. She took a huge risk in challenging an established political machine that had been in place for many years, and she was endangering her own political future by so doing.

Murkowski quickly lost popularity because of other decisions he made while in office. The first of these was appointing his daughter to the Senate. He also cut back popular programs, particularly one that gave senior citizens $250 a month to assist with living expenses. While cutting these funds, Murkowski sought to raise money for a jet plane for his office. He applied for $2 million from the federal government which was denied. He then requested $1.4 million from the state which in turn was denied; then he acquired a line of credit, purchased a jet for $2.6 million, and spent an additional $95,000 for upgrades and repairs as well as $97,600 to train four pilots.[30] In October 2005 the state's commissioner of natural resources, Tom Irwin, questioned Murkowski's secretive meetings with oil companies regarding the proposed natural gas line. Murkowski dismissed Irwin, whereupon, in an action unprecedented in the history of the state government, six other senior members of his department promptly resigned. The incident cost Murkowski support in the legislature and among his constituents.

On October 18, 2005, Sarah Palin announced her candidacy for the office of governor of Alaska. Her brother, Chuck, had encouraged her in this endeavor because he believed the timing was right. Palin's campaign emphasized her grassroots connection with the people of Alaska. The message she disseminated was that she would listen to the concerns and wishes of the state's citizens. She ran a low-budget campaign using wood from snowmobile crates for posters and computer-generated flyers.[31] While she was gaining in popularity, her platform of ethics and transparency was not received well by everyone.

Well-known Alaska columnist and radio host Dan Fagan, a self-identified conservative, fought with and ridiculed Palin at every opportunity. It was the first time that a talk show host had mocked and misrepresented her, but it would not be the last. However, on October 18, 2006, her plan to run a grassroots campaign was announced in her home to members of the press as well as to her friends: "Keeping it simple is my philosophy. . . . My desire is to see small, efficient government that's going to provide the basic services for Alaska, that's shared by the majority of Alaskans. And in keeping it simple, we know that Alaskans, we crave and we deserve leaders who are not going to approach all of our issues with just merely a partisan approach."[32]

On August 31, 2006, the Federal Bureau of Investigation served some 20 search warrants at various locations around the state, including six legislative offices. The raids revealed a federal investigation into alleged statewide corruption that had been under way since at least 2004. This development turned the tide for Palin, and she took office on December 4, 2006. Palin's race for governor of Alaska was no less intense than her bid for mayor of Wasilla had been, yet she once again managed to stand firm in her convictions and wishes to serve the people of Alaska well. According to author Joe Hilley, "More than [on] any single issue, the election results turned on voter assessment of Sarah as a candidate rather than on her command of policy details."[33]

During her tenure in office as governor of Alaska, Palin gained the skill of managing the budget by cutting spending. She posted the governor's jet purchased by her predecessor on the online auction site eBay three times before she eventually sold it directly to a private citizen of Alaska. She fired the governor's chef, who came with the job, a decision that reportedly did not please her children.

The first piece of legislation signed by Governor Palin had many opponents and was considered controversial. Although the state had banned legal gay marriage, the legislation permitted partners of same-sex couples employed by the state the right to receive health benefits. Palin herself does not favor the legality of gay marriage; however, the Alaska Supreme Court had ordered the state to comply with its ruling that benefits be extended to same-sex partners of state employees and retirees by January 1, 2007, just weeks after Palin's inauguration. When she signed the legislation on December 20, Palin provided for an advisory vote already approved by a lame duck session of the legislature in the waning days of Frank Murkowski's tenure as governor. If approved by the voters, the advisory vote could result in the issue going before the electorate in the November 2007 election.[34] Nevertheless, by signing the measure even while publicly objecting to it, Palin prevented a confrontation between the judicial and executive branches of the state government. She subsequently vetoed a bill passed by the state legislature that would have flouted the court's decision, holding that her signature would have been illegal. In the April advisory vote, the proposal to put an amendment banning the benefits before the voters passed by a slim majority, with just a 23 percent turnout, and Palin let the issue drop.

Another major controversy during Palin's tenure as governor of Alaska was the so-called Bridge to Nowhere. The Gravina Island Bridge, which was intended to replace a ferry that connected the island to mainland Alaska, was in the planning stage when Palin took office. It had been a contentious issue because it served only a small portion of the Alaskan population; after Hurricane Katrina struck, Congress suggested diverting the funds to rebuild New Orleans. Governor Palin realized that the state's portion of the funding would increase dramatically if the project were to be continued, and she made the difficult decision to cancel it. Some of her supporters were unhappy about losing the transportation project that they desired.

As governor of Alaska, Palin nonetheless achieved a popularity rating of nearly 90 percent, a feat which is considered to be astounding in politics. And while during all of her political campaigns, "her opponents had more time in public office, more business experience, and more money to spend on their campaigns," yet according to Joe Hilley, "none of that mattered."[35] Palin has the uncanny ability to surround herself with those who are knowledgeable on whatever issues arise and to make wise decisions that represent the best interests of her constituents. Biographer Kaylene Johnson quotes Donald Moore of Wasilla who served as manager of the Matanuska-Susitna Borough for 10 years and has had ample opportunity to observe Sarah Palin's political career: "Sarah is a very gracious woman. But she does not suffer fools."[36]

NOTES

1. Mayer, Jane, "The Insiders: How John McCain Came to Pick Sarah Palin," *New Yorker*, October 27, 2008 (http://www.new yorker.com/reporting/2008/10/27/081027fa_fact_mayer). Accessed on April 16, 2010.

2. Ibid.

3. Transcript: "Gov. Sarah Palin at The RNC: Listen: Sarah Palin's Acceptance Speech," September 3, 2008, http://www.npr.org/templates/story/story.php?storyId=94258995. Accessed on November 4, 2008.

4. "CNN Poll Gives Palin Slight Advantage over Others for 2012 GOP Nomination," http://content.usatoday.com/topics/post/Organizations/Companies/Manufacturing,+Construction/Harley-Davidson/59559020.blog/1.

5. Thornburgh, Nathan, "How Sarah Palin Mastered Politics," *Time*, August 31, 2008, www.time.com/time/politics/article/0,8599,1838572,00.html. Accessed on November 20, 2008.

6. Johnson, Kaylene, *Sarah: How a Hockey Mom Turned the Political Establishment Upside Down* (Carol Stream, IL: Tyndale House Publishers, 2008), p. 41.

7. Ibid., pp. 43–44.

8. Ibid., p. 44.

9. Johnson, Kaylene, *Sarah: How a Hockey Mom Turned the Political Establishment Upside Down* (Carol Stream, IL: Tyndale House Publishers, 2008), p. 45.

10. Thornburgh, Nathan, "How Sarah Palin Mastered Politics," *Time*, August 31, 2008, www.time.com/time/politics/article/0,8599,1838572,00.html. Accessed on November 15, 2008.

11. Ibid.

12. Ibid.

13. Thornburgh, Nathan, "Mayor Palin: A Rough Record, September 2, 2008," http://www.time.com/time/politics/article/0,8599,1837918,00.html. Accessed on October 25, 2008.

14. Ibid.

15. Hilley, Joe, *Sarah Palin: A New Kind of Leader* (Grand Rapids, MI: Zondervan, 2008), p. 54.

16. Ibid., p. 57.

17. Mufson, Steven, "Sarah Palin and Big Oil," *Washington Post*, August 30, 2008, http://newsweek.washingtonpost.com/postglobal/energywire/2008/08/sarah_palin_and_big_oil.html. Accessed on November 15, 2008.

18. Ibid.

19. Ibid.

20. Garber, Kent, "A Look at Palin's Role in Alaska's Big Natural Gas Pipeline Project," *U.S. News & World Report*, September 3, 2008, http://www.usnews.com/articles/news/campaign-2008/2008/09/03/a-look-at-palins-role-in-alaskas-big-natural-gas-pipeline-project.html. Accessed on December 3, 2008.

21. Ibid.

22. Ibid.

23. Palin, Sarah, campaign speech, Lancaster, Pennsylvania, October 18, 2008.

24. Cockerham, Sean, "Ruedrich Resigns Post as Regulator on State Gas and Oil Commission," *Anchorage Daily News*, November 9, 2003, http://www.adn.com/2003/11/08/513772/ruedrich-resigns-post-as-regulator.html.

25. Johnson, Kaylene, *Sarah: How a Hockey Mom Turned the Political Establishment Upside Down* (Carol Stream, IL: Tyndale House Publishers, 2008), pp. 75–77;

26. Ibid., p. 78.

27. Maurer, Richard, "Palin Explains Her Actions in Ruedrich Cast," *Anchorage Daily News*, November 19, 2004, http://www.adn.com/2004/11/19/510276/palin-explains-her-actions-in.html.

28. Johnson, Kaylene, *Sarah: How a Hockey Mom Turned the Political Establishment Upside Down* (Carol Stream, IL: Tyndale House Publishers, 2008), p. 82.

29. Ibid., pp., 83–84.

30. Ibid. pp., 86–87.

31. Ibid. p. 95.

32. Benet, Lorenzo, *Trailblazer: An Intimate Biography of Sarah Palin* (New York: Threshold Books, 2009).

33. Hilley, Joe, *Sarah Palin: A New Kind of Leader* (Grand Rapids, MI: Zondervan, 2008), p. 83.

34. McAllister, Bill, "Gay Partners of State Employees Win Benefits," KTUU-TV, http://www.ktuu.com/Global/story.asp?S=5843150.

35. Hilley, Joe, *Sarah Palin: A New Kind of Leader* (Grand Rapids, MI: Zondervan, 2008), p. 166.

36. Johnson, Kaylene, "The Old Guard Blown Away by Hurricane Sarah Palin, an Unstoppable Force before She Turned Two," *Sunday Times*, September 7, 2008, http://www.timesonline.co.uk/tol/news/world/us_and_americas/us_elections/article4690577.ece. Accessed October 25, 2008.

Chapter 7

LAW AND ORDER IN WASILLA

The frontier culture of Alaska differs from yet is simultaneously similar to that of the Lower 48 states. Hunting and fishing are sports in many rural locations throughout America, and a drinking tradition is typical in these areas. Working people in rural areas use alcohol as a means of relaxation after a long day as well. Rosie Buzzas, a Montana state legislator who also oversees alcohol counseling services in the western part of her state, frames the problem as follows: "There's a church, a school, and 10 bars in every town."[1] Isolation and boredom among teenagers in the long dark winters often contributes to the problem.

In Alaska, in addition to the working-class "party" ethic and boredom factors, migration of Native Alaskans to the big cities has also contributed to many of the problems arising from alcohol abuse. Studies have shown that there is "no evidence that Native Americans possess any greater genetic predisposition to alcoholism than the general population. Alcohol, however, [continues] to take a devastating toll in Indian country."[2] And while the "firewater" that colonists and fur traders gave Native Americans was simply watered-down alcohol heavily spiced with hot peppers to taste more like undiluted alcohol, some

Indian groups chose to use alcohol as part of ritual ceremonies while others distributed it to the entire population.[3]

Today, women and children often suffer from the ramifications of alcohol abuse. According to the website AAANativeArts.com, the FAS (Fetal Alcohol Syndrome) prevalence rate among Alaska Natives is more than triple that for all Alaskans and at least seven times the high end of the national rate of 0.1 to 0.7 percent for the United States as a whole. In a recent survey, the percentage of Alaskan Native mothers who drank during pregnancy was 12.3 percent compared with 1.5 percent for the U.S. population as a whole. The high unemployment rate among Native peoples is often cited as a reason for their reliance upon alcohol: "Unemployment rates in villages are staggering. In one out of every eight villages, unemployment among Native men is in excess of 50%. In one third of all Native villages, male unemployment rates (32%) nearly quadruple statewide average unemployment rates." And extended unemployment often leads to poverty: "25.7 percent of the Alaska Native population earns below the US poverty level standard, compared to 17.8 percent for all races in the U.S. and 9.8% for all Alaskans."[4]

A depressed culture, high poverty levels, difficulty in finding and keeping jobs, and the low self-esteem common among Natives on reservations as well as those survivors of ancient Alaskan peoples living off the land in remote areas of the tundra are indeed factors that play a role in their extreme abuse of alcohol.

Nome, Alaska, home of the Iditarod finish line, is one of the cities with a severe binge-drinking problem. Many of the Natives come into town during the Iditarod event and also at the time that the annual citizen dividend checks from the Alaska Permanent Fund (APF) are distributed each year to Alaskan residents. The APF was established in 1976, when some public lands on the North Slope proved to be an extremely profitable source of oil. Royalties derived from the sale of oil from Alaskan lands are placed in a diversified public trust fund including stocks, bonds, and real estate, and dividends are distributed annually to anyone living in Alaska for a minimum of one year. The first APF dividend checks were mailed to citizens in 1982, in the amount of $1,000 for every citizen resident in the state for at least one year. The dividends have continued to be paid out annually. To date the largest amount paid out was $1,964, in 2000. "The amount changes based on a five-year average of APF investment income derived from the bonds, stock dividends, real estate and other investments."[5]

Nome is a popular spot for heavy drinking among many residents and also individuals from neighboring areas that prohibit alcohol sales or possession. The town is a particular draw to Native American Indians who live on reservations that are usually isolated and "dry" communities. The dangers of alcohol are heightened by the freezing temperatures; incapacitated from too much drinking, people have suffered from frostbite and been killed from exposure to the elements. In Nome, rates of homelessness and crime have been fueled by liquor.

Even prior to the pipeline and the Iditarod, the city of Nome was no teetotaling town: "Nome's boozing history was born with the town after gold was discovered in 1898, bringing thousands of hard-drinking fortune hunters. The gunslinger Wyatt Earp operated the Dexter, the most ornate of 50 saloons lining Front Street in the Gold Rush heyday, when the town's population swelled to 20,000. Nowadays, Nome police officers estimate they spend a third of their time tending to intoxicated people—some repeatedly—and making arrests for drunken driving and such booze-fueled crimes as domestic violence and assault." According to District Attorney John Earthman, alcohol is involved in 90 percent of the 1,000 or so criminal cases around the region that are prosecuted each year.[6]

Alaska recently has been counted among the top 10 most violent states per capita in the United States, and Wasilla "has among the highest per capita violent and property-crime rates in Alaska."[7] At campaign stops, Palin often described Wasilla as a charming, small town, reminiscent of a Norman Rockwell painting. However, in addition to locally owned businesses such as Chimo Guns, the Mocha Moose Café, and the Mug Shot Saloon, the town consists of big-box stores including Wal-Mart, Target, and Lowes, as well as strip malls and fast food chains. Additionally, the town has 11 bars. In short, Wasilla "is an unexceptional, gritty town, bisected by a four-lane highway.... You certainly can have a great time swigging beer in two bars that are allowed to stay open until 5 A.M. It was Mayor Palin who rejected attempts to make them close earlier. If Palin had completely had her way, in fact, you could have sidled up to the bar with a gun."[8] And according to

Mark Jacobson of *New York* magazine, people in Wasilla actually do so.[9] And with this comes the danger of the Wild West in Wasilla: "At the Mug-Shot Saloon, you can memorize the expletives on the collection of bumper stickers next to the well of bottles. But once you leave, you might want to watch your back."[10] In actuality, you are more likely to be assaulted in Wasilla than in Anchorage or in any of the Lower 48 states according to Alaska Demographics.[11]

The need for a Wasilla police force may have its roots in some of the same types of problems although clearly not to the same extent of those experienced in Nome. Anchorage bars are required to close between 2:30 A.M. and 3:00 A.M. Revelers often drive from Anchorage to Wasilla to continue their drinking sprees into the wee hours of the morning. And along with the abuse of alcohol comes the types of crime with which it is associated: muggings, murders, wife beatings, rape, and molestation.

Of importance to note about Wasilla, which was not incorporated until 1973, is that the town did not have a police force until 1993. In fact, Irl Stambaugh was the first police chief in town and the man who built up the department. Prior to Stambaugh's appointment, Wasilla basically had no need for its own force since state troopers were keeping the peace: "The town was patrolled by state troopers, who, sick of making dope and domestic-abuse arrests, told the city to get their own cops. To this end, [Mayor John] Stein, against much opposition, instituted a 2 percent sales tax on goods sold within the Wasilla city limits. This financed a police department."[12] As the town of Wasilla began to grow and develop, crime increased. The sales tax continued to provide the necessary funds to maintain law and order.

Irl Stambaugh had a long history in law enforcement: he had served with the Anchorage Police Department and had earned the rank of captain before he came to Wasilla in 1993. During his first year on the job, he trained eight officers who, within a year, arrested 206 drunk drivers.[13]

But Palin and Stambaugh soon clashed over proposed laws. Stambaugh favored legislation already in place to prohibit the carrying of concealed weapons in bars, banks, and schools, and he actively opposed a National Rifle Association and backed a legislative proposal to loosen these restrictions. In the summer of 1996, he also supported a measure to move up closing time for bars in Wasilla from 5:00 A.M.

to 2:00 A.M., which was intended to reduce drunk driving, domestic violence, and other alcohol-related crimes. As a city council member, Sarah Palin voted with the majority in a 3–2 decision against the ordinance. Supporters of the proposals as well as Stambaugh have argued that Palin opposed the measure because she received support from local bar owners and the National Rifle Association.

Stambaugh remained in office until soon after Sarah Palin replaced John Stein as mayor in December 1996. Because of the provisions of his contract, he did not submit his resignation when Palin asked all of the other heads of city departments to do so, and he was told that Palin would "expect his loyalty." On January 30, he was informed that he had been dismissed. Stambaugh retained a lawyer, and he subsequently sued both Palin and the city for wrongful dismissal.[14]

"Mayor Palin has stated on several occasions that the National Rifle Association encouraged her to fire Chief Stambaugh because of his stance against the concealed weapons legislation," Stambaugh's lawsuit claimed.[15] Palin's view of the subject is somewhat different: She has repeatedly declared that she was facing an old boys' network that had been in place for quite some time. Colleen Sullivan Leonard, a staff member in Palin's office, asserted, "We had a lot of people that were kind of dead wood. We needed people with new energy and a new vision."[16] Palin was clearly well liked by the local pub owners: during her mayoral campaign, one of the bar owners in Wasilla held a fundraiser for her,[17] and she remains a lifetime member of the NRA.

There were some other more personal issues that may have played a part in Palin's decision to fire Stambaugh. A city administrator hired by Palin claimed that Stambaugh had made an offensive remark to her following her mayoral victory: "Little lady, if you think you have our respect, you don't. You have to earn it." (Stambaugh denied having made this remark.) In an affidavit, Palin complained that the Wasilla police had conducted an unauthorized background check on her husband and herself.[18] But of all these reasons for tension between Stambaugh and Palin, perhaps the one most difficult to reconcile was the fact that Palin believed Stambaugh remained loyal to Stein even after she was elected mayor.

Ultimately Stambaugh's lawsuit was unsuccessful; a federal judge determined that Palin had every right to fire and hire staff as she chose.

Stambaugh was replaced by Charlie Fannon, now well known for his opposition to local government in Alaska footing the bill for forensic evidence tests given to rape victims which could cost the town up to $1,000 per kit.[19]

Sarah Palin was a "maverick" in the tundra long before the 2008 presidential campaign. She altered the shape of the Wasilla government to suit what she believed would be in the best interests of her constituents. At the same time, she was an integral part of the hunting and fishing culture that predominates in Alaska. And apparently, she supported the drinking culture as well by permitting some of the bars to remain open until dawn.

While the statistics differ for varying areas in Alaska, the types of crime that occur are often similar. Among the most heinous of them is forcible rape of which Alaska as a whole has the highest rate of all of the 50 United States; Anchorage alone has consistently larger numbers annually than all of the rest of Alaska.[20] Thus the spillover of heavy drinkers from Anchorage into the late-night Wasilla bars might be at least partially accountable for Wasilla's high level of reported rapes.

Until 2000, rape victims in Wasilla paid for their own rape kits. The issue eventually became a public matter and a serious concern for Palin. While she claimed that she was unaware of the fact that there was a policy in place to charge rape victims for the forensic evidence gained during routine post-rape hospital procedures, Wasilla was indeed the only town in the Matanuska-Susitna Valley that insisted that women pay the hospital fees incurred by these tests. In fact, in nearby Palmer, "police chief Laren Zager said that to his knowledge, no sexual assault victim [had] ever been billed by the city of Palmer for an exam to collect evidence of a crime. Zager...said he would never expect a victim to be burdened with the cost of a police investigation."[21]

Some found it questionable that Palin claimed she was unaware of the practice. Yet during the time Palin was mayor, Wasilla was not the only city in Alaska charging rape victims. Experts testified before the legislature that in a handful of small cities across Alaska law enforcement agencies were charging victims or their insurance on a fairly regular basis.[22]

In 2000 the Alaska state legislature passed a bill to prevent victims from being asked to pay for rape kits. Eric Croft, the Democratic state representative who sponsored the legislation, believed that the law was necessary because of Wasilla Police Chief Fannon's position on the issue: "We couldn't convince the chief of police to stop charging them." According to Tara Henry, a forensic nurse in the area, "What I recall is that the chief of police in the Wasilla police department seemed to be the most vocal about how it was going to affect their budget."[23]

According to journalist Jessica Yellin, interviews and reviews of records showed no evidence that Palin was aware that victims and their insurance companies were being charged. However, Judy Patrick, Palin's Deputy Mayor at the time, recalled that Mayor Palin went through the budget in detail: "Palin would review each department's budget line by line and send it back to department heads with her changes." Eric Croft believes that there must have been awareness of the fact on Palin's part: "It's incomprehensible to me that this could be a rogue police chief and not a policy decision. It lasted too long and it was too high-profile."[24] Palin certainly was budget-conscious. There were many budget cuts during her tenure as mayor; remarkably, over that time, she reduced the entire budget by half: "The local hospital sent out the bills, but the town set policy, Mr. Croft noted. That policy was reflected in budget documents that Ms. Palin signed."[25]

Yet once Palin became governor, she began supporting programs for female victims of violent crime. She increased funding for domestic violence shelters, providing $266,200 over the course of two years. A Council on Domestic Violence and Sexual Assault was also reauthorized. These policies clearly indicate the increasing need for services for female crime victims in Alaska and Palin's interest in supporting these programs.

Another issue regarding Palin and law enforcement in Wasilla is the situation known as Troopergate. This labeling of the incident involving the attempted firing of state trooper Mike Wooten and the dismissal of Walt Monegan, commissioner of the Department of Public Safety, conjures up connotations that far surpass the seriousness of the allegations. It brings to mind Watergate during the Nixon Era and the endless hours of televised testimony regarding the corruption of the Nixon administration. It is reflective of the negative exaggeration of events regarding Palin's run for the vice presidency as a woman attempting to break the political glass ceiling at the highest level.

The firing of any civil servant usually requires evidence of some form of misconduct, and it appears that Sarah and Todd Palin may have had good reason to attempt to have Mike Wooten fired from his position. Palin's younger sister, Molly, was embroiled in a bitter custody battle with Wooten, her ex-husband, whom she had married in 2001. Allegations have been made by Sarah Palin that in February 2005 Wooten threatened Palin's father. Wooten allegedly told Molly that her father would "eat a [expletive] lead bullet," a remark that Palin says she and her son overheard on a speakerphone.[26]

The Palins also accused Wooten of committing a variety of illicit acts which were investigated by the Alaska state troopers before Palin became governor. Some of the accusations appeared to be relatively minor, such as drinking a beer in his patrol car and trying to evade a $5 fine at the landfill. Some of the other accusations, however—shooting a moose without a permit, killing a wolf with his snow machine, and using a Taser on his 10-year-old stepson—were more serious in nature.

When Monegan, who had been appointed commissioner by Governor Palin in December 2006 and was now Wooten's boss, took no further action in the case based on the previous investigations, the fact that Wooten already had been disciplined for the infractions and his own findings indicated that there had been no new charges. Todd Palin appeared to be troubled by this. In a January 2007 meeting with Monegan, he cited the moose killing as a criminal act.[27] Although using a stun gun is considered illegal in many states and is restricted in some U.S. cities, apparently using a stun gun on a 10-year-old boy is not a criminal offense in Alaska.

Sarah Palin soon called Monegan concerning the same matter, but she denied pressuring him to fire Mike Wooten even though her aides made many inquiries about him with state officials. If Palin was indeed using her office to deal with a personal family matter, it was clearly in the interest of defending her younger sister, for whom she had always played the role of protector, as well as showing serious concern for the well-being of her parents.

Apparently Palin had other grievances against Monegan whom she fired in July 2008. At an August 2008 press conference, she expressed disappointment with budget issues, recruitment, and Monegan's handling of rural bootlegging. This last complaint, however, conflicts with statements she had made three weeks before the dismissal, when she told local television station KTVA that she thought Monegan would make a great director of the Alcoholic Beverage Control Board. She had approved of his work and suggested he should concentrate his attention in the areas of bootlegging and alcohol abuse. Monegan was also praised by others for his effective work against domestic violence and violence against women.[28] Yet there was another twist to the matter: At one point Molly had taken out a restraining order against Wooten. Monegan himself had been involved in a similar divorce situation and had had a temporary restraining order taken out against him by his estranged wife.[29]

In effect, Troopergate is the subsequent investigation of the role that Sarah and her husband Todd played in this scenario. Both Sarah and Todd were investigated by the Alaska State Legislature regarding the legality of their attempts to have Wooten disciplined or fired. Palin has maintained her innocence. Todd received a subpoena to appear before a grand jury investigating the matter, but he refused (along with five other people) and challenged the subpoena.[30] Since the grand jury did not convene until January 2009, the issue had limited impact on the 2008 political campaign. Nevertheless, the McCain/Palin campaign suffered a setback because the widely reported incident appeared at odds with their attempts to portray her as a political reformer rather than a person with a personal agenda in government.

In any case, Sarah Palin at one time considered Wooten to be a decent upstanding citizen. In January 2000, the year before he married her sister, she wrote a reference letter for him: "I have witnessed Mike's gift of calm and kindness toward many young kids here in Wasilla. I have never seen him raise his voice, nor lose patience, nor become aggitated [sic] in the presence of any child." She considered him to be a "fine role model" who had volunteered in local police and youth auxiliary programs.[31] It wasn't until 2005 that the animosity between Wooten and Palin's family began.

The bipartisan legislative ethics panel concluded its inquiry in October 2008. Among its findings, it determined that Palin exerted no unlawful pressure to fire Wooten; additionally, the report concluded that her dismissal of Monegan was within her legal right as governor although the panel conceded that in addition to budgetary concerns the act was motivated by Monegan's resistance to firing Wooten. Palin and her supporters interpreted the findings as "vindication" and denounced the ordeal as a politically motivated attempt to discredit her.

An editorial in the *Anchorage Daily News* questioned Palin's claim of vindication in the matter of firing Walt Monegan: "In plain English, she did something 'unlawful.' She broke the state ethics law.... They [Sarah and Todd Palin] had no sense that the power of the governor's office carries a special responsibility not to use it to settle family scores.... They had no sense that persistent queries from the governor's office might be perceived as pressure to bend state personnel laws.... Has Gov. Palin committed an impeachable offense? Hardly. Is what she did indictable? No. But it wasn't appropriate, especially for someone elected as an ethical reformer."[32]

Todd Palin, also known as the First Gentleman (or, less formally, the First Dude), has played an unusual supporting role in Sarah's work for the Alaskan government. Todd sat in on reviews of the state budget, has been involved in personnel matters, and has called lawmakers when he or his wife have disagreed with what they have done.[33] Both McCain and Palin received negative press as a result of this during the 2008 presidential election.

Todd Palin conceded that he was involved in Troopergate on some level. During the McCain-Palin campaign, he submitted an affidavit to the investigator, Steven Branchflower, temporarily satisfying the subpoena. Todd stressed Sarah Palin's autonomy as governor of Alaska: "Anyone who knows Sarah knows she is the governor and she calls the shots," he wrote.[34] He clearly worried about Wooten's behavior regarding his own children. Indeed, Todd's complaints were filed with the Commissioner as per procedure: "I make no apologies for wanting to protect my family and wanting to publicize the injustice of a violent trooper keeping his badge.... The real investigation that needs to be conducted for the best interests of the public at large is the Department of Public Safety's unwillingness to discipline its own."[35]

In November 2008, the Alaska Personnel Board, a body composed of three political appointees, released a report detailing its separate investigation into Troopergate. It agreed with the state legislature's findings that Monegan was legally fired but went further to clear Palin of all ethics violations, contradicting the previous investigation's assertion that

Palin exerted undue pressure to have Wooten fired. Governor Palin
remains adamant that she fired Mr. Monegan over a budget dispute.

NOTES

1. Egan, Timothy, "Boredom in the West Fuels Binge Drinking,"
New York Times, September 2, 2006, http://www.nytimes.com/2006/
09/02/us/02binge.html. Accessed on December 19. 2008.

2. *US History Encyclopedia,* "Indians and Alcohol," http://www.
answers.com/topic/indians-and-alcohol. Accessed on December 17, 2008.

3. "Alcohol Laws and the Native America," AAANative Arts.com,
http://www.aaanativearts.com/article1610.html. Accessed on December 20, 2008.

4. Quotations and statistics in this paragraph are drawn from "Facts
about Alaska Natives," AAANative Arts.com, http://www.aaanative
arts.com/alaskan-natives/index.html. Accessed on July 6, 2009.

5. Hartzok, Alanna, "Citizen Dividends and Oil Resource Rents—
A Focus on Alaska, Norway and Nigeria," Earth Rights Institute,
Scotland, PA, http://groundswellusa.org/cdann.htm. Accessed on
December 22, 2008.

6. Associated Press, "In Remote Alaska, Wet Towns Draw Heavy
Drinkers," *USA Today,* September 6, 2007, http://www.usatoday.com/news/
nation/2007-09-06-alaska_N.htm. Accessed on December 21, 2008.

7. Coyne, Amanda, "Where the Bars Are Open Till 5 A.M.,"
Newsweek, September 13, 2008; from the magazine issue dated Sep-
tember 22, 2008, http://www.newsweek.com/id/158769. Accessed on
December 21, 2008.

8. Ibid.

9. Jacobson, Mark, "Sarah Palin's Heaven," *New York,* October 12,
2008, p. 34.

10. Coyne, Amanda, "Where the Bars Are Open Till 5 A.M.,"
Newsweek, September 13, 2008; from the magazine issue dated Sep-
tember 22, 2008, http://www.newsweek.com/id/158769. Accessed on
December 22, 2008.

11. Muni Net Guide, "Wasilla, Alaska," http://www.muninetguide.
com/states/alaska/municipiality/Wasilla.php. Accessed on December 22,
2008.

12. Jacobson, Mark, "Sarah Palin's Heaven," *New York,* October 12,
2008, p. 38.

13. Armstrong, Ken, and Hal Bernton, "Sarah Palin Had Turbulent First Year as Mayor of Alaska Town," *Seattle Times*, September 7, 2008, http://seattletimes.nwsource.com/html/politics/2008163431_palin070. html. Accessed on December 24, 2008.

14. Ibid.

15. Ross, Brian, and Joseph Rhee, "Another Controversy for Sarah Palin," ABC News, September 3, 2008, http://abcnews.go.com/Blotter/ story?id=5713866&page=1. Accessed on December 28, 2008.

16. Ibid.

17. Isikoff, Michael, and Mark Hosenball, "A Police Chief, a Lawsuit and a Small-town Mayor," *Newsweek*, from the magazine issue dated September 22, 2008, http://www.newsweek.com/id/158738/out put/print. Accessed on December 14, 2008.

18. Ibid.

19. Yellin, Jessica, "Palin Charged Women for Rape Exams," CNN News, updated September 22, 2008, http://www.cnn.com/2008/ POLITICS/09/21/palin.rape.exams/. Accessed on December 28, 2008.

20. Rosay, Andre, "Forcible Rapes and Sexual Assaults in Alaska," Alaska Justice Forum, Winter, 2004, http://justice.uaa.alaska.edu/ forum/20/4winter2004/a_rapes.html. Accessed on December 29, 2008.

21. Goode, Jo C., "Knowles Signs Sexual Assault Bill," *Frontiersman*, published on Monday, May 22, 2000, 9:00 P.M. AKDT, and May 23, 2000, http://www.frontiersman.com/articles/2000/05/23/news.txt. Accessed on December 29, 2008.

22. Yellin, Jessica, "Palin Charged Women for Rape Exams," CNN News, updated September 22, 2008, http://www.cnn.com/2008/ POLITICS/09/21/palin.rape.exams/. Accessed on December 28, 2008.

23. Ibid.

24. Ibid.

25. Samuels, Dorothy, "Wasilla Watch: Sarah Palin and the Rape Kits," *New York Times*, September 25, 2008, http://www.nytimes.com/2008/09/ 26/opinion/26fri4.html?em. Accessed on December 27, 2008.

26. Thornburgh, Nathan, "Palin and Troopergate: A Primer," *Time*, September 11, 2008, http://www.time.com/time/politics/article/0,8599, 1840675,00.html. Accessed on December 27, 2008.

27. Matier, Philip, and Andrew Ross, "Official Fired by Palin Bears No Grudge," *San Francisco Chronicle*, September 15, 2008,

http://www.sfgate.com/cgi-bin/article.cgi?f=/c/a/2008/09/15/
BALE12T2N3.DTL&type=printable. Accessed on December 27, 2008.

28. Thornburgh, Nathan, "Palin and Troopergate: A Primer,"
Time, September 11, 2008, http://www.time.com/time/politics/
article/0,8599,1840675,00.html. Accessed on December 27, 2008.

29. Matier, Philip, and Andrew Ross, "Official Fired by Palin Bears
No Grudge," *San Francisco Chronicle*, September 15, 2008, http://
articles.sfgate.com/2008-09-15/bay-area/17157240_1_palin-s-
husband-todd-palin-monegan. Accessed on December 27, 2008.

30. Thornburgh, Nathan, "Todd Palin (Among Others) a No-Show
at Troopergate Hearings," *Time*, September 19, 2008, http://www.time.
com/time/politics/article/0,8599,1842992,00.html?xid=Loomia&utm_
source=feedburner&utm_medium=feed&utm_campaign=Feed%3A+ti
me%2Fpolitics+%28TIME%3A+Top+Politics+Stories%29&loomia_si
=t0%3Aa16%3Ag2%3Ar3%3Ac0.0662235%3Ab18816290. Accessed
on December 29, 2008.

31. Bartholet, Jeffrey, and Karen Breslau, "An Apostle of Alaska,"
Newsweek, September 15, 2008, http://www.newsweek.com/2008/09/05/
an-apostle-of-alaska.html. Accessed on December 20, 2009. This story
was reported by Karen Breslau, Andrew Murr and Mark Hosenball in
Anchorage, Alaska; Suzanne Smalley in St. Paul, Minnesota; Michael
Isikoff, Michael Hirsh, and Daniel Stone in Washington, D.C.; Holly
Bailey with the McCain campaign; and Lisa Miller, Sarah Kliff, and
Katie Paul in New York.

32. *Anchorage Daily News*, "Palin Vindicated? Governor Offers Or-
wellian Spin," October 13, 2008, http://www.adn.com/opinion/view/
story/555236.html. Accessed on December 15, 2008.

33. Yardley, William, "Active Role for Palin's Husband in State
Government," *New York Times*, September 13, 2008, http://www.
nytimes.com/2008/09/14/us/politics/14todd.html. Accessed on December 27, 2008.

34. Associated Press, "Court Refuses to Block Palin Probe," *Los Angeles Times*, October 10, 2008, http://articles.latimes.com/2008/oct/10/
nation/na-trooper10. Accessed on December 27, 2008.

35. Bannerman, Lucy, "Sarah Palin: Troopergate Files Reveal Extent of Todd Palin Access," *Times Online*, October 10, 2008, http://
www.timesonline.co.uk/tol/news/world/us_and_americas/us_elections/
article4916022.ece. Accessed on December 28, 2008.

Chapter 8

CAMPAIGN ISSUES

After the 2008 presidential campaign, both John McCain and Sarah Palin stated in numerous interviews that the economy played an important role in the outcome of the election. The not-so-sudden devaluation of many Wall Street stocks and the $700 billion federal government bailout for mortgage lenders who had irresponsibly issued mortgages to people who realistically couldn't afford them brought about much concern regarding the possibility of another Depression similar to the one precipitated by the stock market crash of 1929.

Alan Greenspan, former chairman of the Federal Reserve Board (1987 to 2006) is best known for his laissez-faire approach to the economy and is the man most Americans regard as a doctor who takes the financial pulse of the nation. His memoir, *The Age of Turbulence: Adventures in a New World* (2007), illustrates how he came to be regarded as the United States' most prominent financial analyst. In a statement before the Joint Economic Committee of the U.S. Congress delivered in June 1999, while he was still chairman of the Federal Reserve, Greenspan said, "While bubbles that burst are scarcely benign, the consequences need not be catastrophic for the economy."[1] He indicated that it was not the crash but the "ensuing failures of policy" that led to the Great Depression. Greenspan suggested that in the event of another crash, his measures could prevent a complete collapse of the economy as they had done in 1987.

According to the *Economist*, however, Greenspan has somewhat altered his views on the situation in the recent economic climate. In the past, Greenspan opposed giving the government additional power. In his recent memoir, however, he indicates that he has had a change of heart and is now convinced that intervention is necessary and the best solution in the current economic climate. He would prefer that financial officials rather than the Federal Reserve be given power to seize companies that by their failure threaten the entire economy. Greenspan's comments preceded some of the political slogans of the 2008 presidential campaign: "'We need laws that specify and limit the conditions for bail-outs [and do so transparently with taxpayers' money] rather than circuitously through the central bank, as was done during the blow-up of Bear Stearns.'"[2] It was Greenspan who, back in August 2007, urged the federal government to assist home owners facing foreclosure, rather than pursue such solutions as "freezing mortgage rates," claiming that the results would be far less damaging.[3]

In her vice presidential debate with Joe Biden as well in several television interviews, Sarah Palin explained how the problems of Wall Street were affecting the entire nation. She stressed the necessity of curing the problem caused by irresponsible lenders. During the 2008 presidential campaign, she repeatedly expressed her opposition to having taxpayers bear the burden for Wall Street's failures.

Like Greenspan, Palin sees a light at the end of the tunnel through governmental intervention, but not the kind initiated by the $700 billion bailout. The bailout program was being negotiated by the Bush administration and Congress during the 2008 campaign and was a hot topic for both John McCain and Barack Obama. The plan called for $700 billion to be made available to buy up distressed mortgages. There was a cap placed on the bill so that no more than $700 billion would be available. The number was considered by some to be in the middle of the range actually necessary to fix the problem. It was estimated that it could take anywhere between $500 billion and $1 trillion to get the economy back on track. Additionally, there was a proposal to provide an $85 billion bailout of American International Group (AIG) and $29 billion to support the merger of Bear Stearns and JP Morgan.

Regarding the Federal Mortgage programs Fannie Mae and Freddie Mac, business journalist David Stout explained the proposal: "The Congressional Budget Office says the federal bailout...could cost $25 billion....The Treasury's involvement in the crisis and the speed with which Congress is responding could...raise the value of those mortgages."[4]

Palin took the position that the government can and should play an important role in the oversight of big business because ordinary people trust their investments, life savings, and insurance policies to these companies which do not always have the average citizen's best interests at heart.

In effect, there is great risk for American taxpayers with the $700 bailout. David Stout takes a nonpartisan view of the situation. He explained the inherent dangers of avoiding action altogether: "Elected officials in both parties became convinced that, while a couple of venerable investment banks could fade into oblivion or be absorbed by mergers, the entire financial system could not be allowed to collapse."[5] The $700 billion bailout plan was passed by the House of Representatives with 263 to 171 votes, and it was signed in early October by President Bush.

Palin's belief is that the Republicans, led by John McCain, could have been a major force in turning around the economy if McCain had been elected president. Yet a nonpartisan approach would most certainly have had the best results: "When we see the collapse that we're seeing today, you know that something is broken and John McCain has a great plan to get in there and fix it....There is a danger in allowing some obsessive partisanship to get into the issue that we're talking about today....It is that profound and that important an issue that we work together on this, and not just let one party try to kind of grab it all or capture it all and pretend like they have all the answers. It's going to take everybody working together on this."[6]

Regarding Fannie Mae and Freddie Mac, Palin focused on the role of lobbyists in shaping Washington's response: "Cronyism—it's symptomatic of the grade of problem that we see right now in Washington and that is just that acceptance of the status quo, the politics as usual.... We've got to put government and these regulatory agencies back on the side of the people."[7] Palin fully supported John McCain's position on the economy because she believed that his experience would make him the best intermediary in an economic crisis.

On August 29, 2008, shortly before the Republican National Convention, Senator John McCain introduced Governor Sarah Palin as his prospective running mate at a Dayton, Ohio, rally. AP Photo/Stephan Savoia.

Palin balanced the budget and provided tax relief in Alaska during her years as mayor of Wasilla and governor of the state, and during the 2008 campaign, she set her sights on doing the same for the United States as a whole. She strongly believed that she would be able to transfer her skills from the state level to the national scene by assisting John McCain in his plan to reverse the economic downturn. She was considered to be a "tough grader" when she criticized Barack Obama's record of legislation in Illinois and Washington: "But listening to him speak, it's easy to forget that this is a man who has authored two memoirs but not a single major law or even a reform, not even in the state senate."[8] But Palin's track record regarding governmental budget management on both the local and statewide level spoke for itself. As mayor of Wasilla, she reduced property taxes by 75 percent while spurring economic growth. As governor, she attempted to sell the corporate jet purchased by her predecessor, Frank H. Murkowski, on eBay but did not succeed. (Despite persistent rumors that she had sold it on the site, a Valdez, Alaska, businessman purchased it independently for

$2.1 million.)[9] As governor, Palin banked Alaska's surplus funds to the extent that the capital budget was slashed from $2.3 billion in 2007 on Murkowski's watch to $1.3 billion in 2008.[10]

During the 2008 campaign, Palin and McCain appeared to be in agreement regarding the $700 billion bailout. McCain summed up their policy in his speech at a campaign rally at Virginia Beach on October 13, 2008: "I'm not going to spend $700 billion dollars [sic] of your money just bailing out the Wall Street bankers and brokers who got us into this mess. I'm going to make sure we take care of the people who were devastated by the excesses of Wall Street and Washington. I'm going to spend a lot of that money to bring relief to you, and I'm not going to wait sixty days to start doing it."[11]

Along the campaign trail, McCain reiterated his plan to the nation. His manner of speaking appealed greatly to many average citizens. During a campaign rally in Downington, Pennsylvania, on October 16, 2008, McCain announced his agenda:

I have a plan to protect the value of your home and get it rising again by buying up bad mortgages and refinancing them so if your neighbor defaults, he doesn't bring down the value of your house with him.

I will protect Social Security so that retirees get the benefits they have earned, and I will bring both parties together to fix Social Security so that it is there for future generations.

I have a plan to hold the line on taxes and cut them to make America more competitive and create jobs here at home."[12]

The grassroots style of campaign that McCain and Palin ran paralleled FDR's approach, and the economic plan in some ways resembled the New Deal, which eventually helped to lift the United States out of the Great Depression.

Before he was inaugurated as president of the United States in 1933, Franklin D. Roosevelt accepted the Democratic nomination with the following words: "I pledge you, I pledge myself, to a New Deal for the American people." His New Deal was, in effect, the legislation that brought about a federally funded and administered economic relief program. FDR targeted banking, industry, and agriculture with new programs to assist businesses in danger of collapse. He provided specific programs for unemployed Americans such as the Tennessee Valley Authority and the Civilian Conservation Corps which provided millions of jobs in public works. Farmers were provided with subsidies to assist in producing crops and in creating the ability for them to raise prices.

Other programs such as the Federal Deposit Insurance Corporation, which was intended to protect the savings of Americans in the event of future banking failures, were instituted. Unemployment insurance and old age pensions were introduced in 1936. Minimum wage and maximum working hours were established by 1938, and trade unions were legalized, giving them the right to organize and collectively bargain with management. While helpful, these measures did not solve all the problems of the Depression. Many believe that it took World War II to fully revive the economy.

Palin's policy paralleled in some ways FDR's plan: her belief that by drilling in the Arctic National Wildlife Refuge and other offshore areas, she would not only create new sources of energy for the country but simultaneously create jobs for many unemployed Americans. Additionally, Palin's support for the completion of the gas pipeline, which would carry natural gas from Alaska's North Slope through Canada to the Lower 48 states, would achieve the same end.

According to journalist Steve Mufson, "Before Republican presidential candidate Sen. John McCain (R-Ariz) changed his position to favor offshore drilling, I asked Palin if there were any place she would consider off-limits to drilling. She said she supports drilling in the Chukchi Sea, where oil companies such as Royal Dutch Shell earlier this year bid to drill, but she wavered on Bristol Bay, which President Bush opened up for drilling early last year. She said that "the fear would be that our very rich fish resources would be put in jeopardy."[13]

In a transcript of a *Time* interview, Palin's position regarding these matters was further explicated:

Up here in Alaska we're sitting on billions of barrels of oil. We're sitting on hundreds of trillions of cubic feet of natural gas onshore and offshore. And it seems to be only the Republicans who understand that companies should be competing for the right to tap those resources, and get that energy source flowing into these hungry markets so that we will be less reliant on foreign sources of energy. In a volatile world, relying on foreign regimes that are not friendly to Americans, asking them to ramp up resource production for our benefit, that's nonsensical. The GOP agenda to ramp up domestic supplies of energy is the only way that we are going to become energy independent, the only way that we are going to become a more secure nation.... but the GOP is going to have to prove to Americans in following weeks that we can safely, responsibly and ethically develop these resources."[14]

Palin's position on obtaining oil from the Alaska National Wildlife Refuge (ANWR) may be summed up as follows: she believes that the potential oil garnered from the area could supply the United States for more than 25 years; while ANWR is located within a 20 million-acre site approximately the "size of South Carolina," with modern drilling techniques the actual drilling area would be less than 2,000 acres, similar to the "size of Dulles Airport," all of which may be viewed as a "2-by-3-foot welcome mat on a basketball court"; during three decades of development in the area, "caribou herds have grown and remained healthy"; finally, the creation of many new jobs for Americans while providing safe energy would improve the economy.[15]

The gas pipeline project is considered by many to be extremely ambitious, and there is clearly some conflict with the interests of the big oil companies: some believe that Palin is simply interested in shifting power and getting a better financial deal for Alaska. Torturous negotiations have been carried on between Alaska's state government and the oil companies for years. Governor Frank Murkowski's support for an agreement offering some assurances on natural gas taxes probably contributed to his defeat in the 2006 Republican gubernatorial primary won by Sarah Palin.

Once elected, Palin had an immediate impact on the protracted negotiations. She "increased tax rates on current oil production, pushed through the Alaska Gasline Inducement Act, which authorized a $500 million subsidy for TransCanada, and increased pressure on ExxonMobil by revoking some undeveloped gas leases on the North Slope."[16] TransCanada claimed Canada's Northern Pipeline Act granted it the right to own and operate the first natural gas pipeline constructed through Canada, but while Sarah Palin was Alaska's governor, the company had yet to secure all of the rights-of-way required. In June 2009, Exxon Mobil joined TransCanada in the pipeline project and began the process to gain the state's approval as a full co-licensee on the project.

A high point of the 2008 vice presidential race was the Commission on Presidential Debates which sponsored a televised debate between candidates Sarah Palin and Joseph Biden held in St. Louis, Missouri, on October 2, 2008. Energy policy and economic issues were on the agenda, as was foreign policy, notably the wars in Iraq and Afghanistan. Both candidates used the occasion to take swipes at the presidential candidates heading the opposing ticket as well as to explain and defend their own positions.

Analysts generally agreed that Palin had held her own against Biden who was well known as an experienced debater.[17] Her successful debate performance nevertheless received less press coverage than the damaging interview with Katie Couric. Palin praised General David Petraeus and criticized Democratic presidential candidate Barack Obama for his position regarding the war in Iraq: "I know that the other ticket opposed this surge, in fact, even opposed funding for our troops in Iraq and Afghanistan. Barack Obama voted against funding troops there after promising that he would not do so," she said, "And Senator Biden, I respected you when you called him out on that."[18] In response, Biden pointed out that, like Obama, John McCain had voted against funding for troops when he disagreed with an amendment attached to the legislation.

Palin also praised her own running mate, McCain, for keeping an open mind about differing opinions, even within his own political party. Framing McCain as a new type of candidate, Palin repeatedly referred to their team as mavericks who had opposed both political parties when "it was time to put partisanship aside and just do what was right for the American people."

Palin has had many critics regarding her lack of information pertaining to international politics. Commenting on Christopher Beam's critical remarks in the online magazine *Slate*, which introduced recommendations from a number of "media trainers" on how Palin could improve her interview performance, Romesh Ratnesar of *Time* magazine characterized Palin's responses in the Katie Couric interview as

Republican presidential nominee Senator John McCain and his running mate acknowledge applause at the Republican National Convention in St. Paul, Minnesota, September 4, 2008. AP Photo/Jae C. Hong.

"hesitant, convoluted and, at times—like when she appeared to suggest that Russian Prime Minister Vladimir Putin might be preparing a one-man airborne invasion of Alaska—downright loony."[19] Kathleen Parker agrees: "Quick study or not, she doesn't know enough about economics and foreign policy to make Americans comfortable with a President Palin should conditions warrant her promotion."[20]

Clearly, Palin is not the first vice presidential nominee to lack an understanding of international affairs. She was open about admitting that she had never met a head of state before September 23, 2008, when she met with certain foreign dignitaries who had come to New York City for a meeting of the United National General Assembly. Spiro Agnew, for example, who served under President Nixon from 1969 through 1973, also had no contact with dignitaries of foreign states before he took office.

However, Steve Biegun, one of Palin's foreign policy advisers, asserted that the true purpose of her meetings in New York was simply to familiarize her with leaders representing America's closest allies. Face-to-face talks would assist her in understanding their perspectives on important international matters.[21] Palin was praised for her ability to develop a rapport with those heads of state: "'Obviously, she was meeting with some people who are very well-established leaders, and her purpose in these meetings was to develop a relationship and listen,' said Biegun, later lauding Palin's skill at establishing a rapport. 'She has a great style.'"[22]

Palin had closed door meetings with President Hamid Karzai of Afghanistan, President Alvaro Uribe of Columbia, the presidents of Georgia and Ukraine, the Indian prime minister, Manmohan Singh, and former U.S. secretary of state Henry Kissinger. It was reported that issues related to trade, drug trafficking, terrorism, and energy were discussed. Journalists who were given brief access to initial or closing exchanges between Palin and the world leaders reported that the vice presidential candidate was well received. At one point, she and Karzai engaged in small talk concerning his son, Mirwais, whose name means "light of the house."

In spite of these meetings during the campaign, Palin's lack of foreign policy experience was evident in comparison to her Democratic counterpart, Joe Biden, who sat for many years on the Senate Committee on Foreign Relations and served as its chairperson. Palin seemed to contradict McCain's position on cross-border attacks by U.S. troops entering Pakistan from Afghanistan to pursue terrorists; she was unfamiliar with the so-called Bush Doctrine of preemptive action. And she cited the threat of Russian incursions into Alaskan air space to shore up her foreign credentials. Nevertheless, many have argued that Palin's experience with oil and natural gas is a credible link to the international arena.

In October 2008, executives from Gazprom, the largest energy company in Russia, came to Alaska to discuss investing in Alaskan energy projects, meeting with the Alaska Department of Natural Resources and representatives of ConocoPhillips, an oil company based in Texas but with investments in Russia and a significant presence in Alaska.

Perhaps the most important aspect of the possibility of Gazprom merging its resources with and gaining profits from the Alaskan gas pipeline (which was not explicitly mentioned at the meeting) is that, according to the *International Herald Tribune*, "Gazprom is exceptionally close to the Russian government, and political and energy analysts think its international business activities are closely coordinated with the Kremlin's foreign policy agenda." Vladimir Putin's successor as president of Russia, Dmitri Medvedev, was chairman of Gazprom before assuming the presidency.[23]

Gazprom's agenda in this matter may be merely financial profit. The meeting drew attention during the campaign because of statements made by Palin in her interview with Katie Couric: "As Putin rears his head and comes into the airspace of the United States of America, where do they go? It's Alaska." A spokesperson for Senator John McCain's presidential campaign said the governor was referring to flights by Russian Air Force planes near the state's borders. She has also remarked, "It is from Alaska that we send those [U.S. fighter jets from Alaskan airbases] out to make sure than an eye is being kept on this very powerful nation, Russia, because they are right there. They are right next to—to our state."[24]

U.S. sources generally discounted any threat from these routine Russian flights. But according to a 2006 article in *Pravda Online*, a nationalist Russian newspaper that has a history tracing back to Communist Russia, "Today the USA is intensively preparing for the further inevitable aggravation of relations with Russia. The widening rift between the two countries can lead to another Cold War which will be much more dangerous than the previous one."[25] The article went on to cite the percentage of ordinary Russians who considered the United States a threat to global security (57%) and to quote statements from various official U.S. sources that were construed as hostile toward Russia.

Next-door neighbors are often more aware than others of events taking place in the backyard. Palin's knowledge of Alaska's tundra, climate, and oil and gas reserves and the close proximity of her home state to Russia may indeed be strong qualifications for handling issues that arise between the United States and Russia in the future.

NOTES

1. "Statement of Alan Greenspan, Chairman, Board of Governors of the Federal Reserve System, before the Joint Economic Committee, United States Congress, June 17, 1999," http://www.house.gov/jec/hearings/grnspn4.htm. Accessed December 24, 2008.

2. "Hire the A-Team," *Economist*, August 7, 2008, from *The Economist* print edition, http://www.economist.com/finance/displaystory.cfm?story_id=11896984 [subscribers only]. Accessed December 23, 2008.

3. Treaster, Joseph B., "Greenspan Urges U.S. to Help Those Facing Foreclosure," *New York Times*, December, 17, 2007, http://www.nytimes.com/2007/12/17/business/17greenspan.html?ref=business. Accessed December 18, 2008.

4. Stout, David, "The Wall Street Bailout Plan, Explained," *New York Times*, September 20, 2008, http://www.nytimes.com/2008/09/21/business/21qanda.html?em. Accessed December 16, 2008.

5. Ibid.

6. "Excerpts from Palin's Hannity Interview—Part I," Fox News Channel's *Hannity & Colmes*, *Time*, http://thepage.time.com/excerpts-from-palins-hannity-interview-part-i/. Accessed on January 7, 2009.

7. Ibid.

8. Annenberg Political Fact Check, "GOP Convention Spin, Part II," September 4, 2008, http://www.factcheck.org/elections-2008/gop_convention_spin_part_ii.html. Accessed January 8, 2009.

9. Yardley, William, "Jet That Helped Defeat an Alaska Governor Is Sold," *New York Times*, August 25, 2007, http://www.nytimes.com/2007/08/25/us/25jet.html. Accessed on January 9, 2009.

10. Campbell, Melissa, "Construction Jobs Drop as Future Funding Begins to Waver," *Alaska Journal of Commerce* July 29, 2007, http://alaskajournal.com/stories/072907/fea_20070729002.shtml. Accessed January 5, 2009.

11. McCain's Prepared Remarks for Virginia Beach, Monday [October 13, 2008], "The Page: Politics Up to the Minute," *Time*, http://thepage.time.com/mccains-prepared-remarks-for-virginia-beach-monday/. Accessed on July 3, 2009.

12. McCain's Prepared Remarks, Downington, Pennsylvania, October 16, 2008, http://www.realclearpolitics.com/articles/2008/10/mccains_remarks_in_downingtown.html. Accessed on January 5, 2009.

13. Mufson, Steve, "Sarah Palin and Big Oil," *Newsweek*, August 30, 2008, http://newsweek.washingtonpost.com/postglobal/energywire/2008/08/sarah_palin_and_big_oil.html. Accessed January 5, 2009.

14. Small, Jay Newton, "Transcript: TIME's Interview with Sarah Palin," August 29, 2008, http://www.time.com/time/politics/article/0,8599,1837536–2,00.html. Accessed on January 7, 2009.

15. Palin, Sarah, "The Case for Drilling in ANWR," http://www.startribune.com/opinion/commentary/38719737.html?page=1&c=y. Accessed on July 3, 2009.

16. Jacobson, Gary, "Sarah Palin's Alaska Pipeline Dream Not Yet a Reality," *Dallas Morning News*, September 5, 2008, http://www.dallasnews.com/sharedcontent/dws/dn/latestnews/stories/090608dnpol palinpipes.1a0b928.html. Accessed on January 3, 2009.

17. CNN Election Center 2008, "Biden Touts Experience, Palin Pushes 'Maverick Record,'" October 3, 2008, http://www.cnn.com/2008/POLITICS/10/02/vice.presidential.debate/index.html. Accessed on January 4, 2009.

18. CNN, Election Center 2008, "Transcript of Palin, Biden Debate," October 3, 2008, http://www.cnn.com/2008/POLITICS/10/02/debate.transcript/. Accessed January 5, 2009.

19. Ratnesar, Romesh, *"Viewpoint:* Sarah Palin's Foreign Policy Follies," *Time*, September 27, 2008, http://www.time.com/time/politics/article/0,8599,1845116,00.html. Accessed on January 7, 2009.

20. Parker, Kathleen, "Palin Problem: She's Out of Her League," *National Review*, September 26, 2008, http://article.nationalreview.com/?q=MDZiMDhjYTU1NmI5Y2MwZjg2MWNiMWMyYTUxZDkwNTE. Accessed January 8, 2009.

21. Baum, Geraldine, "Palin Makes Her Debut on the International Stage," *Los Angeles Times*, September 24, 2008, http://articles.latimes.com/2008/sep/24/nation/na-palin24. Accessed on January 7, 2009.

22. Ibid.

23. Kramer, Andrew E., "Russian Gas Executives Visit Palin's Turf," *International Herald Tribune*, October 15, 2008, http://www.iht.com/articles/2008/10/15/europe/15alaska.php. Accessed on January 3, 2009.

24. Saltonstall, David, "Sarah Palin Defends Her Foreign Policy Experience as Governor of Alaska," *New York Daily News*, September 25, 2008, http://www.nydailynews.com/news/politics/2008/09/25/2008–09–25_sarah_palin_defends_her_foreign_policy_e.html. Accessed January 4, 2009.

25. *Pravda Online*, "Russia and USA to Launch Another Cold War after Their Presidents Leave in 2008," April 17, 2006, http://english.pravda.ru/russia/politics/17–04–2006/79247-cold-war-0. Accessed on January 5, 2009.

AFTERWORD

After the election results were in, Barack Obama and Joe Biden were scheduled for the inauguration, while Palin and her family boarded a plane back home to familiar ground in Alaska. The Democratic ticket was elected with some 52 percent of the popular vote; whatever the Palin factor, the result seemed in large part a referendum on the presidency of George W. Bush. Reportedly Palin wished to speak briefly following Senator McCain's gracious concession speech, but this departure from tradition did not occur.

Disappointment was clearly marked on Palin's face; however, her husband, Todd, appeared considerably relieved to be returning to his job on the North Slope and his familiar daily routines. The last few weeks of the campaign had been brutal: much hoopla surrounded the $150,000 that Palin reportedly spent on her wardrobe. Allegations flew that she wasn't aware that Africa is a continent or didn't know which countries are part of the North American Free Trade Agreement (NAFTA). There were also rumors that she had conflicts with her staff on the campaign trail. Later campaign postmortems were rife with tales of conflict and finger-pointing, most fueled by anonymous sources.

On November 11, 2008, Greta Van Susteren of Fox News was granted an exclusive interview with Sarah Palin, conducted in part in Palin's office in Anchorage and in part at her home in Wasilla. The interview aired nationwide over the course of three days on Van Susteren's evening news program, *On the Record with Greta Van Susteren*. It was evident that Van Susteren's intention was to clarify some of the random defamatory accusations that had been directed at Palin, especially during the final weeks of the presidential campaign.

The public had been informed through various news media that Palin had taken time out of her busy schedule to visit upscale department stores such as Neiman Marcus and Saks to purchase designer clothing, spending the exorbitant amount of $150,000. Palin unequivocally told Van Susteren that she herself did not order the clothes; they had been purchased for her by the Republican National Committee before she arrived on the national scene. Hairdressers and make-up artists from New York had previously been arranged as well. Interestingly, no remarks were made about the dollar cost of Barack Obama's public wardrobe at any time during his campaign.

In December 2009, at the Mall of America in Bloomington, Minnesota, Sarah and Todd Palin greet well-wishers at a book-tour event promoting her newly published memoir, Going Rogue. *AP/Photo/ Andy King.*

Van Susteren thoroughly investigated the remarks made about Africa and NAFTA, which seemed calculated to portray Palin as ill-informed at best and at worst as a woman of little intelligence. After twice grilling an anonymous source who had attended the meeting at which Palin allegedly had revealed her ignorance, Van Susteren was convinced that the supposed incident never occurred. Palin agreed and clarified that she had in fact challenged Obama's statements about NAFTA at that time.

During the interview Palin raised two issues that appeared to be of concern to her: seemingly absurd questions about the identity of the mother of her son Trig and the issue of her banning books during her tenure as mayor of Wasilla. Van Susteren noted that some female journalists had been saying nasty things about her as well. Palin attributed many of these smears to her being an unknown or outsider in Washington during the early stages of the campaign and to "bloggers in their parents' basements talking garbage." She stated that she was without a doubt Trig's mother, and she dismissed the book-banning charge. A widely circulated e-mail listing the books she allegedly wanted banned included Harry Potter books that hadn't yet been published during the time she was mayor. She also asserted that these slurs did not get to her and that her children were capable of handling such misinformation since they had grown up in the political arena and were somewhat used to it. One incident, however, did affect her young daughter, Willow, who, when traveling through Philadelphia had witnessed people wearing crude T-shirts depicting her mother. No mention was made in the interview about the obscene Internet images showing Palin's head on the body of a half-naked woman that circulated early on in the campaign which made light of the seriousness of her political career.

Palin mentioned that she did not believe the cheers of "Sarah, Sarah" at campaign rallies were motivated specifically by support for her but rather that they meant, "We've got a woman on the ticket, we've got this manifestation of progress and change in America." When queried by Van Susteren about her feminism, Palin stated that she is a member of Feminists for Life, a pro-life group that is opposed to abortion. Van Susteren suggested that the abortion issue may have held some women back from supporting her; Palin, however, didn't believe this was the real issue although she did not clarify what she considered the real issue to be. She stated that she encourages open debate in her family and in her political life while making her own beliefs and convictions absolutely clear. When asked about her plans for 2012, Palin remarked that she could not predict the future but said that she would not want to miss an open door that God had provided.

On July 3, 2009, 18 months before the end of her tenure as governor of Alaska, Sarah Palin made headline news once again by announcing that she would shortly leave office and that she would not run for governor the following term. On July 26, she did indeed step down and became a private citizen once again. Lieutenant Governor Sean Parnell took over the office of governor. Initially, it was believed that Palin's reasons for this unexpected move involved minimally nine lawsuits filed against her in Alaska for supposed ethics violations after her return to office following the 2008 campaign. A number of other complaints had been filed before the campaign, primarily involving the Troopergate issue.

Palin startled the media as well as many of her supporters with this move, but those familiar with her plays on the basketball court understood that she knew when to sit it out on the bench and wait for the right time to play. Timing is everything in politics as well as in sports. Speculation about her decision to prepare the ground for a 2012 campaign may have had some substance. USA Today claimed that Palin was stepping down "to avoid an unproductive lame-duck status" in her gubernatorial endeavors and to write a book. According to the Washington Post, Palin was attempting to make political connections in Washington of the sort that would prepare her for a run for the presidency in 2012; in effect, by stepping down as governor, she was freeing up time to position herself on the national political scene, possibly with regard to the upcoming presidential election season.

Palin was indeed working on a book. Initially scheduled for release in the spring of 2010, Palin's memoir, Going Rogue: An American Life, was distributed on November 17, 2009, considerably ahead of its anticipated date of publication. Especially during the early weeks after her resignation as governor, Palin was reported to have worked exceptionally hard at producing the manuscript in record time, assisted by Lynn Vincent, a former Navy air traffic controller as well as a freelance writer and feature editor for an evangelical Christian magazine. According to the

Anchorage Daily News, Palin had received a $1.25 million advance from the publisher, HarperCollins.

Once again, the national pastime of tearing down public figures came into play. Michael Carey, a writer for the *Anchorage Daily News*, asserted that "there is a big something missing from Palin's narrative: the voice of a leader."[1] Mark Kennedy claimed the book contained more lipstick and less pit bull; that is, it appeared to be a rather long campaign speech without much of the spunk of a maverick. Other critics felt that it was a "payback job" for all the abuse she had taken during the campaign but that it nevertheless conveyed the true frontier spirit of Alaska. The *Wall Street Journal*'s Melanie Kirkpatrick wrote that the book illustrated Palin's intelligence: "This is not the prejudiced, dim-witted ideologue of the popular liberal imagination."[2]

Going Rogue rapidly became a best seller and, according to at least one source, a gold mine producing over $12 million. The popularity of the book illustrates that in spite of some down-and-dirty mud-slinging, the American and international public remains fascinated with Sarah Palin, her sudden rise to the national political limelight, and has not lost interest in the career of a woman unremittingly determined to break the glass ceiling of the White House.

In January 2010, Fox News announced that Sarah Palin would join the network as a contributor. Among her subsequent endeavors, Palin appeared on January 12 as a guest analyst on Bill O'Reilly's Fox program *The O'Reilly Factor*, and on April 1 she hosted a television "special" giving her the role of commentator (rather than journalist) on Fox's *Real American Stories*, an occasional series focusing on ordinary people overcoming adversity in their lives. The first episode, which appeared on April 1, 2010, featured the well-known country music performer Toby Keith and, in a special segment, "In Their Own Words," former General Electric chief executive Jack Welch, with Palin hosting and discussing their personal challenges and successes. Several other guests joined Palin to tell their stories. "In Their Own Words" was to have featured rapper LL Cool J as well, but before the program aired, he objected to Fox's use of old footage on the program, and his segment was dropped. Keith likewise was reportedly taken aback by the use on the program of an older interview with him that was the property of Fox, but his segment aired as scheduled.

Some claimed that *Real American Stories* would replace Greta Van Susteren's *On the Record*, the broadcast in which Van Susteren had so consistently championed Palin's rise to national prominence. *On the Record* was preempted by the *Real American Stories* broadcast on April 1, yet Van Susteren's program actually followed Palin's segment at 10 P.M. Van Susteren, who holds two law degrees and is considered to be among the world's 100 most powerful women according to *Forbes* magazine, received the 2000–2001 Sandra Day O'Connor Medal of Honor from Seton Hall University and the American Bar Association Presidential Award for "Excellence in Journalism" (2001).

On March 26, Discovery Communications announced that *Sarah Palin's Alaska*, an eight-part series about Palin's home state, would air on its TLC cable network. No specific date was set, but the series, produced by Mark Burnett Productions, was to begin filming in summer 2010. Palin is slated to act as an outdoor guide to her home territory, the great Alaskan landscape. Palin and Burnett were reported to receive $1 million per episode which would make the series one of the most expensive nature programs ever produced. Palin remarked that her family likes watching nature documentaries, and thus she had no qualms about appearing on it.

Bill O'Reilly told Sarah Palin that she was welcome to appear on his show anytime, and future episodes of *Real American Stories* also seem likely. Given its price tag, *Sarah Palin's Alaska* is certain to be well promoted and will keep Palin squarely in the eye of the American public, including viewers who may not regularly tune in to Fox News. Palin's multiyear contract with Fox may, as some commentators have speculated, preclude a run for high elective office in 2012, but it seems safe to assume that it will continue to build and possibly enhance Palin's public platform.

NOTES

1. Carey, Michael, "A Woman Who Savors a Fine Whine," *Los Angeles Times*, November 18, 2009, http://articles.latimes.com/2009/nov/18/news/OE-CAREY18. Accessed on August 19, 2010.

2. Kirkpatrick, Melanie, "Her Side of the Story," *Wall Street Journal*, November 16, 2009, http://online.wsj.com/article/SB100014240527 4870443180457453788268108904.html?mod=WSJ_hpp_sections_opinion. Accessed on August 19, 2010.

Appendix A

INAUGURAL ADDRESS OF GOVERNOR SARAH PALIN, DECEMBER 4, 2006

Surely the warm heart of Alaska is in the Carlson today. I thank you so much for that toasty welcome. This is an honor. Welcome, all.

To our state constitution framers, we honor you. Past and present officials from across the land, we're grateful for you. I thank all our former governors who have served, all of them. And to my family, our big family, I love you. Y'all cleaned up real well today. I don't see a Carhartt in the bunch.

Especially to all you students, thank you for skipping school. Thank you for being here.

I am so glad you are all here, and Libby Riddles, first woman to win the Iditarod. When I was a college student outside in the 1980s, my roommates plastered their dorm walls with pictures of Madonna and Magic Johnson and Metallica. Adorning my walls, truly inspirational, were pictures of Libby Riddles. She was an underdog. She was a risk taker, an outsider. She was bold and tough. Libby, you shattered the ice ceiling. Thank you for plowing the way.

From Kaylene Johnson, *Sarah: How a Hockey Mom Turned the Political Establishment Upside Down* (Carol Stream, IL: Tyndale House Publishers, 2008), 139.

I am humbled to be here with so many good Alaskans in the land of great Native heritage. Alaska is a family. And Alaska Natives, you're the first family. Your embrace welcomed newcomers to this frontier yesterday. It lets us move forward in unity today with respect, with good stewardship of the land of your birth. We're blended. Let us be united with one heart.

Fifty years ago here in Fairbanks, at the Alaska Constitutional Convention, those wise providential pioneers gathered, wrote, and birthed the newest, biggest, richest-in-resources state in the Union with the document that shall guide me as governor.

It demands that Alaskans come first. It will keep my compass pointed true north. It's the tool to build Alaska with strength and with order. Their brilliant document, the constitution, is austere. It concentrates clearly on resource development for our people and is eerily prophetic. Today, although we stand on the threshold of a new frontier, these pioneers still speak to us from the past.

At the start of the convention, delegate Bob Bartlett said he saw two distinct futures for Alaska: one of wise resource management leading to wealth and industry, the other of servitude stemming from loss of control over our resources leading to despair. They had a choice of which route to go as we do today—regress or progress. There's no part of the world where the people and the land fit as they do here. Our nature resources are our lifeblood and are commonly owned by all of us. We are unlike any other state in the Union.

Here, the people are in charge. We have rights and responsibilities to produce. Done right, we see vitality, we fund services, we make a more secure America. And we see opportunities for jobs, for work, and that should be our goal because man was created to work.

Our founding documents then were shaped to fulfill promises that we be self-sufficient and self-determined with a special understanding of the relationship of Alaska and her people to her lands and her water and her wildlife. Bartlett instructed those delegates, saying, "This moment is critical in our history. The future and well-being of our present and unborn citizens depend on wise administration of these developmental activities."

Bartlett was warning against being exploited by outside interests because we were so resource rich. He said, "The taking of our resources without leaving a reasonable return to support needed services will mean a betrayal in the administration of the peoples' wealth. The danger is that competing interests determined to stifle development here, which might compete with activities elsewhere, will acquire our lands in order to not develop it until such time as, in their omnipotence in pursuit of their own interests, they see fit. If our opportunities are squandered, the people of Alaska may be even more the losers than if the land had been exploited."

Wow, the state of the state being what it is today as we embark on gas-line negotiations tomorrow, Bartlett's words spoken nearly a decade before I was born could have just as easily been the content of this morning's newspaper editorial. So, understanding the gravity of that warning, fifty-five heroes wrote strong and clear powers into our state's fine blueprint. It's that ink that will guide me in taking Alaska boldly toward our birthright.

I will unambiguously, steadfastly, and doggedly guard the interests of this great state as a mother naturally guards her own—like a southeast eagle and her eaglet, or more appropriately here in the Carlson, like a nanook defending her cub. Our state, our lands, our future are in our hands.

The most important issue today, as Lieutenant Governor Sean Parnell said, is developing energy supplies, building the foundation upon which we will progress our role internationally. Central today are natural-gas needs. We must tap reserves and explore for more to energize our homes, our businesses, for new industry to come alive, to heat our economy, and allow us self-sufficiency while gifting our nation with domestic supplies. Couple this with Arctic National Wildlife Refuge oil and inexhaustible alternative energy sources, Alaska can lead the nation in a much-needed energy plan to secure these United States, to create a safer world. Why not Alaska fueling the nation? Why not Alaska leading the world? These are perilous times in our world.

America is looking for answers. She's looking for a new direction. The world is looking for a light. It's former Alaska governor Walter Hickel, who reminded me that "that light can come from America's great North Star—it can come from Alaska." It can happen only if we work together in true partnerships and work with our legislators, not against them, putting aside political pettiness and crushing corruption. This is our opportunity to show a new direction.

We can show a new direction, and we can inspire the world. So, I take with me tomorrow our constitution to gas-line negotiations and work with global partners and independents to market our gas. We're in a position of strength here, but that strength comes not from my hand; it comes from what I hold in my hands. Let's be vigilant with competing interests if they encroach on our sovereignty or divide us or force us from opportunity.

We've learned lessons about competing interests. Sometimes it's involved our own federal government. Take fishing, a quick example. First, we'll manage wildlife for abundance—enough for all. I need Alaskans, though, working together when federal decisions adversely affect us. Regions, races, user groups, gear groups must unite in battle for Alaska's right to harvest and to develop. Robust fishers should revitalize coastal communities left in the wake of allocation decisions that mirror fishing issues from fifty years ago that kept us beholden to outside interests when we lived under federal orders that favored a privileged few. So, we sought statehood to control our resources and for fairness. Not going backwards, I oppose contradictions to competition and free enterprise that hurts Alaskans.

Our constitution explains all this—wildlife, oil, gas, minerals, timber, and access for our maximum benefit. Alaska is vast enough for all, plus tourism and technology and university research—all means of creating honest prosperity. We've got great opportunity today even with changes on the national scene. With our congressional delegation in the minority right now, obviously we must prudently consider state priorities as our relationship with federal-funding streams change. Don't fear, though, perhaps delayed dollars coming in. Instead, let us make our wealth outof the wilderness and make our living on the land and on the water. Let's use our hands to build and our minds to lead the nation in innovative advancements.

Governor Hickel said he "never feared an economic depression so much as a depression of the spirit." This is a time to be courageous, not fearful. We must progress. We have to progress to fund public safety and infrastructure and education.

As I focus on natural resources, know that I won't overlook our greatest resource—our children. Our kids deserve the best in education. So, with fresh perspective in schools and K–12 putting parents back at the head of the education family, recognizing that they must guide children, empowering them via school involvement and choices, we can reengage with prospects of success, and I know as a parent, as the guide, I know it's easier to say than to do—believe me.

I believe in public education. I'm proud of my family's many, many years working in our schools. I hope my claim to fame, believe it or not, is never that I'm Alaska's first female governor. I hope it continues to be, "You're Mr. Heath's daughter. My dad for years has been teaching in the schools, and even today he's inspiring students across the state. So many students around this land came up to me not saying, "Oh, you're Sarah Palin ... you're running for office ... you're the governor." No, it's been, "Sarah Palin, wow! Mr. Heath's been my favorite teacher of all time."

Our teachers are our inspiration. We'll provide for successful public schools. I'll treat alternative schools with respect and with enthusiasm because, in fact, every child is worth it. We'll replicate winning re-form so more kids are prepared for work, and we don't import our work force. Much reform won't cost more; it's a matter of priorities so more money gets into the classrooms. Our task is great but so worthy because I won't accept our 40 percent high school dropout rate, nor our lowest college-preparedness rate. That's not success. That's unacceptable. We must do better prioritizing. Students must be answerable and schools held accountable and our good teachers treasured for edifying our most precious resource, those kids. I'm excited to work with the schools to help each child find purpose and know their worth, because everyone has great purpose. Getting kids on the right path, enabling them to be productive citizens—that's our goal together—in a safe environment.

That's another core constitution intent—public safety. We've got to take it back and make every community safer and healthier. Preventing crime and substance abuse relates to family and culture strength and also depends on a vibrant economy. We know the positive effect of em-ployment. It's been said that idle hands do the devil's work. Well, to get idle hands to work, we teach, and through vo-tech training, we refill workforce deficits and we sway young Alaskans to stay and to improve themselves and to improve their state.

So, fifty years ago, this constitution captured a visionary dream filled with promise. Around this gift was a ribbon in the form of a resolution so relevant today. I was reminded this morning by President Mark Hamilton of the University of Alaska as he shared what the resolution said.

It said, "You are Alaska's children. We bequeath you a state that shall be glorious in her achievements, a homeland filled with opportunity for a living, a land where you can worship and pray—an Alaska that will grow as you grow. We trust you. You are our future. Take tomorrow and dream. You'll see visions that we do not see. We are certain that in capturing today for you, you can plan and build. Take our constitution. Study it. Work with it. Help others appreciate it. You are Alaska's children."

I accept this resolution on your behalf, on behalf of all Alaskans. Our sourdoughs and cheechakos, our proud military, our rugged hunters and outdoor enthusiasts, our academics and artisans, all who live in the last frontier and make it exceptional. For you, I rededicate support for our foundation.

I will defend our values. I'll show fiscal restraint to not burden our children with debt and deficit. I'll support competition and free enterprise. I'll insist on ethics in government. I will respect you. I will put Alaska first.

I ran for governor not thinking myself better than anyone, but offering opportunity for the mantle of leadership to be passed. It is time. That torch is fanned with new energy but was ignited long before by pioneers with a responsible, confident vision that I share. Its radiance won't let us lose sight of true north.

Alaskans, hold me accountable, and right back at you! I'll expect a lot from you, too. Take responsibility for your family and for your futures. Don't think you need government to take care of all needs and to make decisions for you. More government isn't the answer because you have ability, because you are Alaskans and you live in a land where God, with incredible benevolence, decided to overwhelmingly bless you.

I'll help you with opportunities. I ask for your continued support in this for Lieutenant Governor Sean Parnell and me. And I ask that you join us in seeking God's wisdom, grace, and favor on Alaska. I thank you all and I thank my family for their amazing support and the responsibilities that they now have ... Girls? Thank you for sharing your mom—Bristol, Willow, and Piper—and our son, Track, who's outside playing hockey this year. I wish that he were in the Carlson today. Todd, thank you. I love you. Thank you for everything.

Alaskans, I am grateful for you and for your warm heart. Alaska's new team cannot wait to get to work for you. We love Alaska, and God bless you all.

Appendix B

ADDRESS OF THE VICE PRESIDENTIAL NOMINEE TO THE REPUBLICAN NATIONAL CONVENTION, SEPTEMBER 3, 2008

Mr. Chairman, delegates and fellow citizens: I am honored to be considered for the nomination for Vice President of the United States...

I accept the call to help our nominee for president to serve and defend America.

I accept the challenge of a tough fight in this election...against confident opponents...at a crucial hour for our country.

And I accept the privilege of serving with a man who has come through much harder missions...and met far graver challenges...and knows how tough fights are won—the next president of the Unites States, John S. McCain.

It was just a year ago when all the experts in Washington counted out our nominee because he refused to hedge his commitment to the security of the country he loves.

"Remarks as Prepared for Delivery by Alaska Governor Sarah Palin," at the 2008 Republican National Convention, St Paul. Transcript available online from the *New York Times*, http://elections.nytimes.com/2008/president/conventions/videos/transcripts/20080903_PALIN_SPEECH.html (accessed August 26, 2010). Reprinted with permission from the Republican National Committee.

With their usual certitude, they told us that all was lost—there was no hope for this candidate who said that he would rather lose an election than see his country lose a war.

But the pollsters and pundits overlooked just one thing when they wrote him off.

They overlooked the caliber of the man himself—the determination, resolve, and sheer guts of Senator John McCain. The voters knew better.

And maybe that's because they realize there is a time for politics and a time for leadership...a time to campaign and a time to put our country first.

Our nominee for president is a true profile in courage, and people like that are hard to come by.

He's a man who wore the uniform of this country for twenty-two years and refused to break faith with those troops in Iraq who have now brought victory within sight.

And as the mother of one of those troops, that is exactly the kind of man I want as commander in chief. I'm just one of many moms who'll say an extra prayer each night for our sons and daughters going into harm's way.

Our son Track is nineteen. And one week from tomorrow—September 11th—he'll deploy to Iraq with the Army infantry in the service of his country.

My nephew Kasey also enlisted and serves on a carrier in the Persian Gulf.

My family is proud of both of them and of all the fine men and women serving the country in uniform. Track is the eldest of our five children.

In our family, it's two boys and three girls in between—my strong and kind-hearted daughters Bristol, Willow, and Piper.

And in April, my husband Todd and I welcomed our littlest one into the world, a perfectly beautiful baby boy named Trig. From the inside, no family ever seems typical. That's how it is with us. Our family has the same ups and downs as any other...the same challenges and the same joys.

Sometimes even the greatest joys bring challenge. And children with special needs inspire a special love. To the families of special-needs children all across this country, I have a message:

For years, you sought to make America a more welcoming place for your sons and daughters. I pledge to you that if we are elected, you will have a friend and advocate in the White House.

Todd is a story all by himself. He's a lifelong commercial fisherman... a production operator in the oil fields of Alaska's North Slope...a proud member of the United Steel Workers Union...and world champion snow machine racer. Throw in his Yup'ik Eskimo ancestry, and it all makes for quite a package.

We met in high school, and two decades and five children later, he's still my guy.

My Mom and Dad both worked at the elementary school in our small town. And among the many things I owe them is one simple lesson: that this is America, and every woman can walk through every door of opportunity.

My parents are here tonight, and I am so proud to be the daughter of Chuck and Sally Heath.

I know just the kind of people that writer had in mind when he praised Harry Truman. I grew up with those people. They are the ones who do some of the hardest work in America ... who grow our food, run our factories, and fight our wars. They love their country, in good times and bad, and they're always proud of America.

I had the privilege of living most of my life in a small town. I was just your average hockey mom, and signed up for the PTA because I wanted to make my kids' public education better.

When I ran for city council, I didn't need focus groups and voter profiles because I knew those voters, and knew their families too.

Before I became governor of the great State of Alaska, I was mayor of my hometown.

And since our opponents in this presidential election seem to look down on that experience, let me explain to them what the job involves.

I guess a small-town mayor is sort of like a "community organizer," except that you have actual responsibilities. I might add that in small towns, we don't quite know what to make of a candidate who lavishes praise on working people when they are listening, and then talks about how bitterly they cling to their religion and guns when those people aren't listening. We tend to prefer candidates who don't talk about us one way in Scranton and another way in San Francisco.

As for my running mate, you can be certain that wherever he goes, John McCain is the same man.

I'm not a member of the permanent political establishment. And I've learned quickly, these past few days, that if you're not a member in good standing of the Washington elite, then some in the media consider a candidate unqualified for that reason alone.

But here's a little news flash for all those reporters and commentators: I'm not going to Washington to seek their good opinion—I'm going to Washington to serve the people of this country. Americans expect us to go to Washington for the right reasons, and not just to mingle with the right people.

Politics isn't just a game of clashing parties and competing interests. The right reason is to challenge the status quo, to serve the common good, and to leave this nation better than we found it.

No one expects us to agree on everything. But we are expected to govern with integrity, good will, clear convictions, and ... a servant's heart.

I pledge to all Americans that I will carry myself in this spirit as vice president of the United States. This was the spirit that brought me to the governor's office, when I took on the old politics as usual in Juneau, when I stood up to the special interests, the lobbyists, big oil companies, and the good-ol' boys network.

Sudden and relentless reform never sits well with entrenched interests and power brokers. That's why true reform is so hard to achieve. But with the support of the citizens of Alaska, we shook things up. And in short order we put the government of our state back on the side of the people.

I came to office promising major ethics reform, to end the culture of self-dealing. And today, that ethics reform is the law.

While I was at it, I got rid of a few things in the governor's office that I didn't believe our citizens should have to pay for.

That luxury jet was over the top. I put it on eBay. I also drive myself to work.

And I thought we could muddle through without the governor's personal chef—although I've got to admit that sometimes my kids sure miss her. I came to office promising to control spending—by request if possible and by veto if necessary.

Senator McCain also promises to use the power of veto in defense of the public interest—and as a chief executive, I can assure you it works. Our state budget is under control. We have a surplus.

And I have protected the taxpayers by vetoing wasteful spending: nearly half a billion dollars in vetoes.

I told the congress "thanks, but no thanks," for that Bridge to Nowhere. If our state wanted a bridge, we'd build it ourselves.

When oil and gas prices went up dramatically and filled up the state treasury, I sent a large share of that revenue back where it belonged—directly to the people of Alaska.

And despite fierce opposition from oil company lobbyists, who kind of liked things the way they were, we broke their monopoly on power and resources.

As governor, I insisted on competition and basic fairness to end their control of our state and return it to the people.

I fought to bring about the largest private-sector infrastructure project in North American history. And when that deal was struck, we began a nearly forty-billion-dollar natural gas pipeline to help lead America to energy independence. That pipeline, when the last section is laid and its valves are opened, will lead America one step farther away from dependence on dangerous foreign powers that do not have our interests at heart.

The stakes for our nation could not be higher. When a hurricane strikes the Gulf of Mexico, this country should not be so dependent on imported oil that we are forced to draw from our Strategic Petroleum Reserve. And families cannot throw away more and more of their paychecks on gas and heating oil.

With Russia wanting to control a vital pipeline in the Caucasus, and to divide and intimidate our European allies by using energy as a weapon, we cannot leave ourselves at the mercy of foreign suppliers.

To confront the threat that Iran might seek to cut off nearly a fifth of world energy supplies...or that terrorists might strike again at the Abquaiq facility in Saudi Arabia...or that Venezuela might shut off its oil deliveries...we Americans need to produce more of our own oil and gas.

And take it from a gal who knows the North Slope of Alaska: we've got lots of both.

Our opponents say, again and again, that drilling will not solve all of America's energy problems—as if we all didn't know that already. But the fact that drilling won't solve every problem is no excuse to do nothing at all.

Starting in January, in a McCain-Palin administration, we're going to lay more pipelines...build more nuclear plants...create jobs with clean coal...and move forward on solar, wind, geothermal, and other alternative sources.

We need American energy resources, brought to you by American ingenuity and produced by American workers.

I've noticed a pattern with our opponent. Maybe you have, too. We've all heard his dramatic speeches before devoted followers. And there is much to like and admire about our opponent. But listening to him speak, it's easy to forget that this is a man who has authored two memoirs but not a single major law or reform—not even in the state senate.

This is a man who can give an entire speech about the wars America is fighting and never use the word "victory" except when he's talking about his own campaign. But when the cloud of rhetoric has passed... when the roar of the crowd fades away...when the stadium lights go out, and those Styrofoam Greek columns are hauled back to some studio lot—what exactly is our opponent's plan? What does he actually seek to accomplish, after he's done turning back the waters and healing the planet? The answer is to make government bigger...take more of your money...give you more orders from Washington...and to reduce the strength of America in a dangerous world. America needs more energy...our opponent is against producing it.

Terrorist states are seeking nuclear weapons without delay...he wants to meet them without preconditions.

Al-Qaeda terrorists still plot to inflict catastrophic harm on America...he's worried that someone won't read them their rights? Government is too big...he wants to grow it. Congress spends too much... he promises more. Taxes are too high...he wants to raise them. His tax increases are the fine print in his economic plan, and let me be specific.

The Democratic nominee for president supports plans to raise income taxes...raise payroll taxes...raise investment income taxes...

raise the death tax... raise business taxes... and increase the tax burden on the American people by hundreds of billions of dollars.

My sister Heather and her husband have just built a service station that's now opened for business—like millions of others who run small businesses. How are they going to be any better off if taxes go up? Or maybe you're trying to keep your job at a plant in Michigan or Ohio... or create jobs with clean coal from Pennsylvania or West Virginia... or keep a small farm in the family right here in Minnesota.

How are you going to be better off if our opponent adds a massive tax burden to the American economy? Here's how I look at the choice Americans face in this election.

In politics, there are some candidates who use change to promote their careers. And then there are those, like John McCain, who use their careers to promote change. They're the ones whose names appear on laws and landmark reforms, not just on buttons and banners, or on self-designed presidential seals.

Among politicians, there is the idealism of high-flown speechmaking, in which crowds are stirringly summoned to support great things. And then there is the idealism of those leaders, like John McCain, who actually do great things. They're the ones who are good for more than talk... the ones we have always been able to count on to serve and defend America. Senator McCain's record of actual achievement and reform helps explain why so many special interests, lobbyists, and comfortable committee chairmen in Congress have fought the prospect of a McCain presidency—from the primary election of 2000 to this very day.

Our nominee doesn't run with the Washington herd. He's a man who's there to serve his country, and not just his party. A leader who's not looking for a fight, but is not afraid of one either.

Harry Reid, the Majority Leader of the current do-nothing Senate, not long ago summed up his feelings about our nominee. He said, quote, "I can't stand John McCain."

Ladies and gentlemen, perhaps no accolade we hear this week is better proof that we've chosen the right man. Clearly what the Majority Leader was driving at is that he can't stand up to John McCain. That is only one more reason to take the maverick of the Senate and put him in the White House.

My fellow citizens, the American presidency is not supposed to be a journey of "personal discovery." This world of threats and dangers is not just a community, and it doesn't just need an organizer.

And though both Senator Obama and Senator Biden have been going on lately about how they are always, quote, "fighting for you," let us face the matter squarely.

There is only one man in this election who has ever really fought for you... in places where winning means survival and defeat means death... and that man is John McCain. In our day, politicians have readily share much lesser tales of adversity than the nightmare world in which this man, and others equally brave, served and suffered for their country.

It's a long way from the fear and pain and squalor of a six-by-four cell in Hanoi to the Oval Office. But if Senator McCain is elected president, that is the journey he will have made. It's the journey of an upright and honorable man—the kind of fellow whose name you will find on war memorials in small towns across this country, only he was among those who came home.

To the most powerful office on earth, he would bring the compassion that comes from having once been powerless... the wisdom that comes even to the captives, by the grace of God... the special confidence of those who have seen evil, and seen how evil is overcome.

A fellow prisoner of war, a man named Tom Moe of Lancaster, Ohio, recalls looking through a pin-hole in his cell door as Lieutenant Commander John McCain was led down the hallway, by the guards, day after day. As the story is told, "When McCain shuffled back from torturous interrogations, he would turn toward Moe's door and flash a grin and thumbs up"—as if to say, "We're going to pull through this." My fellow Americans, that is the kind of man America needs to see us through these next four years.

For a season, a gifted speaker can inspire with his words.

For a lifetime, John McCain has inspired with his deeds.

If character is the measure in this election... and hope the theme... and change the goal we share, then I ask you to join our cause. Join our cause and help America elect a great man as the next president of the United States.

Thank you all, and may God bless America.

SELECTED BIBLIOGRAPHY

BOOKS

Benet, Lorenzo. *Trailblazer: An Intimate Biography of Sarah Palin* (New York: Threshold Books, 2009).

Conroy, Scott, and Shushannah Walshe. *Sarah from Alaska: The Sudden Rise and Brutal Education of a New Conservative Superstar* (New York: Public Affairs, 2009).

Heilemann, John, and Mark Halperin. *Game Change: Obama and Clintons, McCain and Palin, and the Race of a Lifetime* (New York: Harper, 2010).

Hilley, Joe. *Sarah Palin: A New Kind of Leader* (Grand Rapids, MI: Zondervan, 2008).

Johnson, Haynes, and Dan Balz. *The Battle for America 2008: The Story of an Extraordinary Election* (New York: Viking 2009).

Johnson, Kaylene. *Sarah: How a Hockey Mom Turned the Political Establishment Upside Down* (Carol Stream, IL: Tyndale House Publishers, 2008).

PERIODICALS

ABC News. "Excerpts: Charlie Gibson Interviews GOP Vice Presidential Candidate Sarah Palin," http://abcnews.go.com/Politics/

Vote2008/Story?id=5789483&page=2. Date of publication: September 13, 2008.

Abcarian, Robin. "Sarah Palin's College Years Left No Lasting Impression," *Los Angeles Times*, October 21, 2008, http://www.latimes.com/news/nationworld/nation/la-na-palincollege21-2008oct21,0,2546859,full.story.

Armstrong, Ken, and Hal Bernton. "Sarah Palin Had Turbulent First Year as Mayor of Alaska Town," *Seattle Times*, September 7, 2008, http://seattletimes.nwsource.com/html/politics/2008163431_palin070.html.

Bartholet, Jeffrey, and Karen Breslau, "An Apostle of Alaska," *Newsweek*, September 15, 2008, http://www.newsweek.com/id/157696/output/print.

CBS *Evening News*, Anchor Katie Couric Interviews Alaska's Governor on the Ailing Economy, "One-On-One With Sarah Palin," New York, September 24, 2008, http://www.cbsnews.com/stories/2008/09/24/eveningnews/main4476173.shtml.

CNN Election Center 2008, "Biden Touts Experience, Palin Pushes 'Maverick Record,'" October 3, 2008, http://www.cnn.com/2008/POLITICS/10/02/vice.presidential.debate/index.html.

Davey, Monica, "Little Noticed College Student to Star Politician," *New York Times*, October 24, 2008, www.nytimes.com/2008/10/24/us/politics/24palin.html.

Fox News Channel's "Hannity & Colmes," "Excerpts from Palin's Hannity Interview—Part I," *Time*, http://thepage.time.com/excerpts-from-palins-hannity-interview-part-i/. Accessed on January 7, 2009.

Garber, Kent, "A Look at Palin's Role in Alaska's Big Natural Gas Pipeline Project," *U.S. News & World Report*, September 3, 2008, http://www.usnews.com/articles/news/campaign-2008/2008/09/03/a-look-at-palins-role-in-alaskas-big-natural-gas-pipeline-project.html.

Isikoff, Michael, and Mark Hosenball, "A Police Chief, a Lawsuit and a Small-town Mayor," *Newsweek*, from the magazine issue dated September 22, 2008, http://www.newsweek.com/id/158738/output/print.

Lafferty, Elaine, "Sarah Palin's a Brainiac," *Daily Beast,* www.the dailybeast.com/blogs-and-stories/2008–10–27/sarah-palins-a-brainiac/1/—94k. Date posted: October 27, 2008.

Matier, Philip, and Andrew Ross, "Official Fired by Palin Bears No Grudge," *San Francisco Chronicle,* September 15, 2008, http://www.sfgate.com/cgi-bin/article.cgi?f=/c/a/2008/09/15/BALE12T2N3.DTL&type=printable.

Meyer, Jane, "The Insiders: How John McCain Came to Pick Sarah Palin, *New Yorker,* October 27, 2008, http://www.newyorker.com/reporting/2008/10/27/081027fa_fact_mayer.

Mufson, Steven, "Sarah Palin and Big Oil," *Washington Post,* August 30, 2008, 11:18 A.M., http://newsweek.washingtonpost.com/post global/energywire/200.

Saltonstall, David, "Sarah Palin Defends Her Foreign Policy Experience as Governor of Alaska," *New York Daily News,* September 25, 2008, http://www.nydailynews.com/news/politics/2008/09/2008–09–25 sarah palin defends her foreign policy e.html8/08/sarah palin and big oil.html.

Small, Jay Newton, "Transcript: TIME's Interview with Sarah Palin," August 29, 2008, http://www.time.com/time/politics/article/0,8599,1837536–2,00.html.

Thornburgh, Nathan, "How Sarah Palin Mastered Politics," *Time,* August 31, 2008, http://www.time.com/time/politics/article/0,8599,1838572,00.html.

INDEX

About the Author

CAROLYN KRAEMER COOPER has been a college writing instructor for over 25 years at major New York State universities, including the City University of New York, St. John's University, and the State University at New Paltz. She is currently freelancing as both a writer and a photographer. Her work has been published in *Yoga Journal*, *The Journal of Religion and Health*, the *Rivertowns Enterprise*, and the online publication The Examiner.com. She has been the recipient of the David Markowitz Award for Poetry and has received honorable mention in the De Jur Writing Contest for poetry. This is her first published biography.